RELIGION
IS NOT DONE
WITH YOU

RELIGION IS NOT DONE WITH YOU

OR, THE HIDDEN POWER OF RELIGION ON RACE, MAPS, BODIES, AND LAW

MEGAN GOODWIN AND
ILYSE MORGENSTEIN FUERST

BEACON PRESS, BOSTON

BEACON PRESS
Boston, Massachusetts
www.beacon.org

Beacon Press books
are published under the auspices of
the Unitarian Universalist Association of Congregations.

27 26 25 24   8 7 6 5 4 3 2 1

This book is printed on acid-free paper that meets the uncoated paper
ANSI/NISO specifications for permanence as revised in 1992.

Text design and composition by Kim Arney

Library of Congress Cataloging-in-Publication Data is available for this title.
ISBN: 978-0-8070-1275-8; e-book: 978-0-8070-1276-5-;
audiobook: 978-0-8070-1722-7

To our dads,
our first and forever audience

And to Kathleen Marie Foody,
Best Quality Sister

CONTENTS

INTRODUCTION So You Think You're Done with Religion ▪ 1

CHAPTER 1 Religion Is (Not) Baseball ▪ 19

CHAPTER 2 Religion Is Global ▪ 35

CHAPTER 3 Race Is (Made of) Religion ▪ 66

CHAPTER 4 Religion Is Politics ▪ 96

CONCLUSION Religion Is a Flight Risk ▪ 119

HOMEWORK What Do You Do with the Religion
That Is Not Done with You? ▪ 146

Acknowledgments ▪ 154
Index ▪ 157

RELIGION
IS NOT DONE
WITH YOU

SO YOU THINK YOU'RE DONE WITH RELIGION

*in which we start by explaining who we are,
why we care about religion,
and why you should—and will—too*

R eligion? Really? In this economy?

Look, we get it. We mean, come on. It's the twenty-first century. Religion is cute for your nana, or if your favorite TV show introduces a vampire or a hot priest or a vampire hot priest or something. But, surely, in real life, nobody actually does that stuff anymore.

Right?

Here's the thing: religion shapes the world around us, whether you're doing religion or not. Have you ever been admitted to a hospital? Gotten married or tried to adopt? Been to court? Gone through airport security? Used a map? Voted?

Do you use a calendar?

We regret to inform you that religion shapes how (and whether) you do any of those things—regardless of how you personally feel about religion. And if you don't have the tools to recognize religion at work, it can be very hard to see, much less understand, those connections, making it darn near impossible to see how religion shapes the world around us.

The bad news is most folks don't have a chance to study religion academically, if they ever get to study it at all. (That, by the way, is also a consequence of how religion has shaped the world around you. We'll come back to this.) The good news? We're here to help.

ARE YOU DONE WITH RELIGION?

Fear not! We're not interested in making you religious—or, if you're already doing religion, in telling you how to do it right or better. Being done with religion (or not) is a deeply personal issue for lots of folks. The ways we think (or don't) about religion get shaped by how we were raised, where we are now, how we and our commitments and our goals have changed over time. Maybe you have a robust religious life in community with folks who share your values and worldview. Maybe you'd like to do more but you haven't quite found your place yet.

You might be a deeply spiritual person who doesn't resonate with traditional or organized religion. Or you might be an atheist or a free-thinker and you know beyond a shadow of a doubt that this is all there is.

Maybe you think religion used to matter, but we're really past that sort of thing by now (or should be)—that obviously religion is important to some people but mostly humans have, like, evolved past all that—and you can't figure out why other people's religions seem to get talked about so much, especially around election times. Or maybe you're ambivalent. You don't even care whether or not you care, because who cares, you know? Or maybe you care very deeply about religion, because to you, religion means politics and war and violence and hate and oppression, and maybe if we fixed religion we could fix the rest of this mess, too.

All of these are completely valid ways to feel about religion. Seriously. You get to feel about religion however you want. Honestly, that's all you. God(s) bless. Or not! Any way you feel about religion is fine by us.

But—and it's a big but—how you feel about religion is only the tiniest bit of why religion matters. And we care very much that you know that. Because *not* knowing that religion infuses and informs every part of our world? That's dangerous, and it allows a lot of unnecessary and violent oppression to flourish. We need you to know that *even if you're done with religion, religion is not done with you.*

Which is why we wrote this book.

WHO THE HECK ARE WE?

We know you've probably heard that religion isn't an appropriate thing to talk about in public. So why are we talking about it? Why are we telling *you* to talk about it? Why should you listen to us? Who do we think we are, anyway?

So glad you asked.

We *think* we're funny, but we *know* more about religion than most folks. We both have master's degrees and doctorates in religion (Megan in gender, sexuality, and American religions; Ilyse in Islam, race and racialization, and South Asia). We actually met as grad students in the University of Chapel Hill's Department of Religious Studies in 2007 and have been thinking and talking about religion together ever since. We've both written books and lots of articles on religion, taught dozens of religious studies classes, won grants and awards to research religion, given interviews and authored op-eds and delivered public talks on religion. We love thinking—and talking to each other—about religion so much that we created a podcast about it! And that award-winning podcast led directly to this very book.

Thinking and writing and talking about religion are our day jobs, but religion is also a central part of our personal lives. Both of us belong to minority religious communities. We are religious people who—in very different ways and for deeply different reasons—care about justice and repairing our broken world.

Professionally, Ilyse's work centers on Islam, race, and imperialism. She cares a lot about how racial systems mesh with religious ones. Her writing and teaching always focus on how race, religion, and power are always, always in the room. But Ilyse was also adopted at birth by an Ashkenazi Jewish couple who raised her in a fairly progressive synagogue in New Jersey (to which her lingering accent attests); she watched the Twin Towers fall on television during her first week of college, minutes after leaving a class about religion. All of those things shape her commitments to social justice, racial equity, queer and feminist spaces, and dismantling systems of Christian oppression. She's a mom of two killjoys-in-training, a frequent complainer to various powers that be about calendars (we'll get there; wait for it), and someone with a knack for explaining global patterns—like that old telephone commercial, her line is: it's all connected. Ilyse is also a multiple-award-winning teacher, so projects like this—where we explain a phenomenon and then try to puzzle through what to do next—are her favorite.

Megan's work focuses on race, gender/sexuality, politics, and American minority religions—including groups many people call "cults," even though she has begged them not to. A self-described stone cold bummer, Megan centers her research and teaching on oppressive American systems rooted in excluding and disciplining religious, racial, gender, and sexual outsiders. She's a loud large queer disabled neurodivergent ginger lady raised by Philadelphia Catholics who, inspired by Pat Buchanan, infamous white Christian nationalist and political advisor, decided to leave the church of her youth to date women, critique capitalism, and practice witchcraft instead of having children. Megan is a pro-queer antiracist feminist dedicated to helping students, listeners, and anyone else who'll listen realize that religion is a force for change—not always bad, not inherently good, but always changed and changing.

With their powers combined, Ilyse and Megan have spent the last fifteen years conspiring to build chosen family (Megan is an aunt to Ilyse's small humans), foment social justice, talk religion, teach our students and listeners and readers, and kill joy in the radical hope that life-giving change can come from it.

"Killjoy" might sound negative, and certainly some folks use the word that way. For us, being killjoys means combining our academic training and personal commitments to think clearly and carefully about how religion works in the world: all the damage people do in the name of religion, and all the creativity, joy, resistance, and survival that religion makes possible.

We borrow the term "killjoy" from renowned feminist and antiracist scholar Sara Ahmed. In *The Promise of Happiness* (2010), Ahmed says that "to kill joy is to open a life, to make room for life, to make room for possibility, for chance." For us, being killjoys isn't about telling people they're dumb or wrong for not thinking about religion the way that we do. Being killjoys means calling out bullshit takes on religion: takes that insist religion is always and everywhere good *and* takes that want to write religion off as irrelevant, irrational, or regressive. We want to use our personal and professional experiences to help folks recognize religion at work, to see that *not* talking about religion hasn't kept it from shaping our lives. If our world needs work—and we sure think it does—that work starts with being able to name and understand the forces that undergird our systems. This book, we hope, makes room for possibility, for chance, for more ways of being safely different in the world.

Now that you know who we are, let's get into this book you're holding.

WHAT THE HECK IS THIS BOOK?

We wrote this book in part as a companion volume to our hit podcast, *Keeping It 101: A Killjoy's Introduction to Religion.* If you're already a listener: you know we love you, and we're happy you're here to learn even more about religion. If you want to become a listener or just be reminded of what to listen to: we make suggestions for further listening in each chapter, giving you reading/listening pairs that go together like a fine wine with a stinky cheese or a short Jewess with a large loud gingeress (if we don't say so ourselves).

And if you're not a podcast person at all, that's just fine! This book has lots to teach you about religion no matter what you put in your ears, and it stands apart from the work we've done on *Keeping It* 101. As long as you're asking the right questions, there's no wrong way to learn about religion.

Let's begin with the rightest question: Why should you care about religion? We've said it before, many times, many ways, but whatever and however you feel about religion, *religion is not done with you*.

This isn't to say that you, your feelings, or your opinions don't matter. Of course they do. In fact, your relationship to religion matters quite a lot! And so does the fact that schools, courts, businesses, and media outlets have encouraged you to assume religion is only as important as it is important to *you, personally.*

Sure, you have the choice to participate in religion or not. But *how* you make that choice builds on your entire personal history, your connection to communities and regions, and the systems that surround you. All of which—as we're here to show and tell you—have been shaped by religion. Religion shapes what choices you get to make: what you can learn in school, how your government works, what kind of options you have (or increasingly don't have) in caring for your own body. Heck, even the way we tell time is shaped by religion!

Religion is systems and structures and assumptions we didn't create or choose—and, to be honest, we might not even like or agree with. We think you and your choices matter very much. The systems that organize our societies, on the other hand, could not give less of a care about you or your individual choices. You can feel however you want to feel about religion, but religion is shaping your world whether you like it or not. And if you *don't* like how religion is shaping our world? This book might just be your first step in diagnosing the problems and agitating for positive change.

Religion Is Not Done with You can show you, dear reader, how religion—that messy, complicated, amazing, often frustrating series of overlapping and sometimes contradictory systems—functions. We'll show you how certain ways of being in the world came to be called "religious," how what we now call "religion" has changed over time and place, what people do with religion, and how religion works in our homes, our communities, our nations, our world.

Maybe you're done with religion. Maybe you're not. But either way?

Religion is not done with you.

WHAT THE HECK IS RELIGION, ANYWAY?

We keep using this word "religion" like maybe it does not mean what you think it means. But hold up, we hear you saying. Doesn't everybody already know what religion means? Religion is about belief, and books, and special buildings, and special days and seasons, and how I feel, and maybe a historical founder who might or might not wear a funny hat. And, yes, religion is about all of those things! Some of the time! But religion isn't *just* those things, and it's not always those things, either. Religion, as you might be realizing, is a big old mess.

James Baldwin thought so too, by the way. In "Letters from a Journey" (1965), he asked, "*What*, precisely, is a religion? And how dreary, how disturbing, to find oneself asking, now, questions which one supposed had been answered forever! But one is forced to ask these kindergarten questions."

We sure are, Mr. Baldwin, because religion means *so many things*. Like foodways! Language practices! The concepts of whiteness and race, period, as we now understand it in the United States! And then there's all the vague uses of religion—the ways it sometimes means "the Boston Red Sox are my religion," or "I watch *Love Island UK* religiously," or "Beyoncé's tour was a religious experience." Religion sometimes means those things, too.

Religion has way too many uses, too much history, too many con-flicting goals for a flashcard definition. Sorry. But just because religion is hard to define doesn't mean we can't—or shouldn't—define it.

Religion is, as we like to say, what people do. And it turns out people are a big old mess. We mean, have you *met* people? They're a big, wonderful, terrible, overwhelming, exhausting, irreplaceable mess. So it makes all the sense in the world that people, who are a damn mess, make messy religion and religious messes.

Yes, when we're talking about religion, we *are* talking about prayers, and rituals, and leadership, and morality, and fancy build-ings, and maybe funny hats or special kinds of underwear. But we're also talking about why kosher food usually can only be found in its own aisle, often the "ethnic" aisle, in the supermarket; why we vote on Tuesdays in the US; and where our understandings of race and gender and sexuality come from. No matter what else we're talking about, though, when we're talking about religion, we are always . . .

Always . . .

ALWAYS . . .

talking about power.

Learning to talk about religion requires learning how to see and name the roots of our legal, medical, educational, juridical, cultural, literary, and linguistic systems—the systems that make us who we are, whether we recognize their influences or not.

HOW DO WE TALK ABOUT RELIGION?

When it comes to talking about religion, it's all about the doing. Doing religion can mean participating in formal rituals like pujas or bat mitzvahs or salat*—but it can *also* mean your Irish Catholic nana

---

* Puja is a South Asian worship practice performed by Hindus, Jains, and Buddhists. Bar, bat, b'nai and b mitzvahs are Jewish coming-of-age ceremonies. *Salat* (or *salah* or *namaz*) refers to Muslim prescribed daily prayer rituals.

sprinkles you with holy water if she thinks the devil has you acting up. (Not that this ever happened to one of us.) Doing religion can mean being in community with people who share your commitments, even if they also sometimes drive you bonkers. Doing religion changes over time and place; doing religion means a lot of different things to a lot of different people. And folks who study religion—that's us!—take seriously *all* the ways people do religion.

There's an old joke that if you have three Jews in a room you'll have twice as many opinions. Judaism sees *itself* as being open to debate, interpretation, and change. There are, of course, different ways to be Jewish in the world. There are official branches, like Orthodox, Reform, Conservative, Reconstructionist, and Hasidism, among others. But lots of different kinds of Jews practice lots of different kinds of Judaism in lots of ways that don't fit neatly into these "proper" designations.

You probably know that *kashrut* (Jewish dietary law) forbids observant Jews to eat pork. But we also know—some of us might even be related to—Jews who nosh BLTs. If your inner Judge Judy wants to say, unacceptable, Jews aren't allowed to have bacon and therefore the Jew who eats bacon is a *bad Jew* or a *lesser Jew* or *not a Jew at all*, we are going to need you to (1) hush; only Judy can judge us and (2) remember: *religion is what people do*. BLTs or no BLTs, a Jew is someone who claims Jewishness and is claimed as a Jew by others (Jewish or otherwise). Judaism is what Jews do—all of them, not just the ones you like—because religion is what people do.

Religion isn't a list at the club; we're not checking to see who's allowed in the VIP room. Other folks might be in the business of background checks and qualifying exams. If you're a rabbi, for example, your literal job might include defining proper practice and appropriate Judaism. But we're religious studies scholars, not religion cops. We're not keeping people out; we're asking questions about human complexity. And the question here isn't "Is Ilyse's bacon cheeseburger-eating mom *really* Jewish?" It's "How does Judaism somehow include *both* kashrut *and* Ilyse's mom?" Because it does. And thank goodness.

It is *not* our job to tell people doing religion that they're wrong about their own lives, experiences, rituals, beliefs, or practices. For people who study religion, it's our job (and this "our" includes you now, since you're reading this book) to make sense of that tension, that seeming paradox.

Studying religion is all about exploring contradictions. Why are there so many freaking translations of the Bible? How can religious communities that preach equality and love support hurtful policies? If Hinduism is polytheistic, how come some Hindus only interact with a handful of gods? If Islam is a global religion, and most Muslims speak languages that aren't Arabic, why is Arabic so important to so many Muslims? If Judaism prohibits bacon, why does Ilyse's Jewish mom love it crispy?

The answer to all these questions is the same: because people are messy, and religion is what people do. Religion is what people do with their histories, memories, relationships, and, yes, texts (sometimes) and bodies (always) in particular locations and time periods. If we start with "religion is what people do" and remember that people are messy, alive, and always changing, we *expect* that religion is messy and alive and always changing, too. Our job isn't to police religious belonging—our job is just to try to keep up with all the many millions of ways people are doing religion.

Oy vey, you exclaim! Is *everything* people do religion, then? Well: yes, and also no, and maybe skip ahead to chapters 2 and 3 for more on this. But the short answer is *both* that religion does an awful lot *and also* that, no, not everything people do is religion. If religion were a basketball, you wouldn't need this book; you would just be able to see it, name it, throw it around. The basketball. Not this book. Please don't throw this book. We worked hard on it.

WHAT WE TALK ABOUT WHEN WE TALK ABOUT RELIGION

Aren't we supposed to avoid talking about religion, though? Isn't religion-talk improper or rude, especially in mixed company? Maybe for you religion is intensely private—a relationship between you and the Divine, the Universe, a god or God—and talking about it feels like a violation of that sacred, private connection. And that's fine! It's fine to be private about your own religiosity or lack thereof. It's fine to talk about how you feel about religion so long as the folks you're talking with consented to have that conversation.

But if you've read this far, you already know that religion is far more than a personal relationship. Religion is what people do, and religion offers us a framework for understanding why and how people do what they do.

We invite you to get curious about *why* some of us are taught to assume being polite—being civil—means not talking about religion in public. Hint: treating religion as special and private and frankly rude to even mention is a pretty effective way to hide systems of power in plain sight.

We think naming injustice and disrupting inequality outweigh "civility." If we're too worried about offending each other with religion-talk, we can never even begin to address Islamophobia and its impacts on Muslims and Sikhs alike. If we avoid conversations about religion and politics at dinner tables, we'll never understand, much less disrupt, how much "secular" Western law, policy, and diplomacy hinges on white conservative Christian understandings of morality.

We, and especially those of us who are located in the Global North, who are white, and/or who are Christian, are *especially* encouraged to render religion invisible, unspeakable, internal, and ultimately dismissible as a special interest rather than a foundational social force. We are trained not to see religion, not to talk about religion, not to make our religion other people's business. This disappearing act matters because making religion about identity politics makes it almost impossible to recognize or address religion at work in our systems.

The folks who want you not to talk about religion are the folks whose religious worldviews are winning (even if they don't recognize them or claim them as religious worldviews. We see you, France). Do you want hordes of unvaccinated, angry, and armed white folks storming the US Capitol to "save America" from people and policies they consider immoral? Because you get Capitol sieges by spending two-hundred-plus years telling folks that everyone else's religion is none of their business and then use white Christian worldviews to structure society at every conceivable level. You make white Christian assumptions and morality so much the norm that people don't even recognize them as Christian anymore—that's just good old American values. And if you try to extend legal protections or even just plain old human dignity to people who fall outside those "values"? You get senators hiding under their desks, Confederate flags flown in the seat of US government, and some crusty old white dude's feet up on Nancy Pelosi's desk.

Look, we told you religion was messy.

WE HAVE TO TALK ABOUT RELIGION

Keeping religion unspeakable allows intolerance and inequality to flourish. If we can't see religion at work, we can't understand white supremacy, or misogyny, or classism, or ableism. A just world requires us to name religion when it fosters Islamophobia, antisemitism, and anti-Black racism in the name of national security or American values. And learning to see religion at work helps us recognize the potential of religion—and the people who use it—to work toward a kinder, safer, better world.

Talking about religion helps us learn that religion is systems, traditions, communities, and worldviews. Heck, religion is a big part of where countries and borders come from. Religion is how we got Europe. Also the Americas. (We'll come back to this, too; please hold for chapter 3.) Religion is complicated, enraging, contradictory, uplifting, dangerous, beautiful, exhausting, overwhelming—because people, who do religion, are all those things and more.

We probably don't have to tell you that people use religion to do terrible things to one another. As we write, Islamophobic rhetoric, violence, and laws are on an unprecedented rise all over the world. Anti-Muslim hate crimes in North America are at their highest point since September 2001. Antisemitic hate crimes are the highest they have ever been in the US. North American anti-Asian hostility is contributing to unprecedentedly high rates of anti-Sikh, anti-Hindu, and anti-Buddhist crimes. Arsonists are targeting Black churches. Native people are losing sacred lands to environmentally devastating business interests. There are life and death consequences to religion.

But religion also shapes smaller parts of our lives—parts we might not even recognize as having anything to do with religion. Have you felt religious using a mindfulness app? Do you think about doing yoga as doing religion? Why are so many folks identifying as "spiritual but not religious" or "nones" these days, and what does that even mean?

We have to talk about religion because not talking about religion lets injustice flourish. But not talking about religion also means missing out on incredible expressions of human creativity. So we're going to help you learn how to talk about religion: help you build up your vocabulary; flex your critical thinking brain-muscles; and give you some examples to share with other folks who might be interested in this conversation.

SO ARE YOU *SURE* YOU'RE DONE WITH RELIGION?

Hopefully by now you're pretty sure that you're *not* done with religion. But where should you start looking for it?

Ilyse loves to say that religion lurks in the floorboards—it's *there*, *waiting*, even if you think you've swept up well, even if you think your home can be free from the outside culture's use of religion. (Megan likes to say that this makes religion sound like the telltale heart from that Edgar Allan Poe story. Which is creepy—but not inaccurate?) For example, did you know that . . .

Religion is in your yoga class?!

Yoga is freaking everywhere these days, right? You can't cruise down any Main Street without passing a yoga studio. Elementary school teachers are using yoga to help unruly little kids control their unruly little bodies. "Yoga pants" are the pandemic "soft pants" choice of many; there are whole industries—and multilevel marketing schemes—built around selling you the right sort of leggings to do intentional stretching in. Businesses and insurance companies are offering "mindfulness" as a universal solvent for burnout and exhaustion. Two separate medical professionals literally prescribed yoga to Ilyse—like, on a prescription pad—as treatment for chronic pain. (Spoilers: deep breaths can't fix the violence of white-supremacist cis-het patriarchal ecoterrorist capitalism.)

None of this explains what yoga is doing in this book, though. What does yoga have to do with religion? Oh, friends, we are so very glad you asked.

Yoga is now a multibillion-dollar global industry, but it started as a specific type of Hindu ritual practice. Yoga originated as a way to physically and ritually discipline the bodies of high-caste Hindu men. In fact, "yoga" literally means "discipline"—*religious* discipline that very old, very sacred Sanskritic texts, like the *Bhagavadgita* and *Pātañjalayogaśāstra* (Patañjali's Authoritative Exposition of Yoga) required of Brahmin men to the exclusion of nearly all others.

So how the heck did yoga start as a high-caste men-only ritual practice and wind up next to paint-your-own-pottery stores and frozen yogurt stands in your local strip mall? Thinking about all the changes, movements, and interpretations this Sanskritic, Hindu, Brahmin (and male-dominated) physical discipline had to go through for that to happen blows our fragile little minds.

But fun facts and thought experiments aren't why we're asking you to rethink yoga. We want you to see how white Western businesses were able to successfully and profitably lift yoga's stretching and breathing and muscle-building out of its religious and cultural context and sell it back to us as mindfulness and exercise—without making most of us think twice about appropriation, globalization, colonialism, or white supremacy.

The de-religion-ing of yoga is part exploitation, part admiration, part imperialism, part scientific "progress," and part so-called secularization. For now, we'll just say that this book will help you think about whose religion gets recognized, protected, and honored as "religion" and whose religion gets violently suppressed only to be sold back to white ladies ages eighteen to forty-five by Nike, Urban Outfitters, the Calm App, and Lululemon.

Does this mean you can't do yoga anymore? No, it does not. Heck, Ilyse even does her prescription yoga as part of physical therapy. She's mad about it—both because physical therapy hurts and because she thinks the commodification of non-Western ritual practices is gross and exploitative—but she's doing yoga nonetheless. And so can you! But if you keep reading, we promise you're going to notice a lot of messiness around supposedly secular institutions and organizations.

So, if yoga isn't your scene, do you still have to care about religion? We're afraid so, friends. Because:

Religion is in your healthcare system?!

Picture it: You're in a horrific car wreck. You're pregnant. You've been badly injured and knocked unconscious. Someone calls an ambulance. State law requires that ambulance to take you to the nearest trauma 1 response center. Treatment that could save your life risks terminating your pregnancy.

You are in danger, and not just for the reasons you might expect.

You are in danger because this trauma center (despite its innocuous and seemingly secular name) is owned by a corporation that is owned by the Roman Catholic Church—as are so, so many hospitals and healthcare facilities throughout the United States, particularly in rural and impoverished regions. The care this trauma center will provide for you depends *not* on what your doctor thinks is best for you, but on what care the Catholic organization that owns the center thinks is moral and proper for you to receive.

You might be an atheist, a deeply religious Jew, or a committed Muslim; your personal religious commitments might morally provide for the need to end a pregnancy to save the life of the parent. But the hospital does not have to and *will not* take your personal relationship to religion into consideration when determining your course of care. The facility has to default to the position of the Roman Catholic Church, which means no action can be taken to preserve the life of the child or parent over the other.

The trauma center you did not choose, whose morality does not reflect your own, gets final say about how—even whether—they decide to save your life. The stakes of religion not being done with you are, in this case, literally life and death.

Other people's religion is all up in your reproductive business. Recent Supreme Court cases—*Burwell v. Hobby Lobby* (2014) and *Little Sisters of the Poor Saints Peter and Paul Home v. Pennsylvania* (2020) for example—undermined the contraceptive mandate in the Affordable Care Act. Simply put, this means that nine mostly Catholic mostly white mostly men decided that a business owned by people who by their own admission do not understand the difference between birth control and abortion get to decide whether their employees can safely and reasonably access contraception—regardless of individual employees' own relationships to religion. Hobby Lobby and any other "closely held corporation" (if you're asking yourself what that means, don't worry, so are a million lawyers) doesn't have to subsidize birth control for any and all Muslim, Jewish, or atheist employees, even though those employees' religions or lack thereof morally permit contraceptive use.

The Supreme Court of the United States of America made corporations people (*Citizens United* [2010]), extended religious freedom protections to those corporation-people (*Hobby Lobby* [2014]), and now US corporations do not have to pay their fair share toward their employees' healthcare if that healthcare includes contraception. All so some science-denying pipecleaner peddlers can control the bodies of their employees. Because, you know, religion.

We'll get back to religion and healthcare in chapter 4. But what if you're not into yoga and you've been lucky enough not to need reproductive healthcare? Do you still have to care about religion? 'Fraid so, friends. Because

Religion is in TIME ITSELF?!?!?!?!!

Pull out your phone from your pocket, please, and click your calendar app.

Mazel tov, you've found religion in your pants.

The standard calendar preloaded into smart phones is the Christian calendar. The year the world "agrees" on—better put, the year that white Christian imperialists imposed the world over (more on *this* in chapter 2 and the homework)—is a year that literally honors how many years have passed since the birth of Jesus Christ, a famously not-Hindu, not-Muslim, not-Buddhist, and shockingly born-Jewish but non-Jewish figure/God.

The red-letter dates on your calendar app may vary by country, but in the multicultural, multireligious North America and Europe, Muslim, Jewish, Hindu, Buddhist, Sikh, and Native or Indigenous holidays are *never* standard. Christmas always is, though. Because in a system based on how many years have passed since Jesus was born, Jesus's birthday is, of course, a given.

The literal way we order our *time*—the one resource none of us can get more of—is rooted in religion. Not just religion! Christianity. A specific religion. Oh! And not just *all* Christianity, a specifically white Protestant version (because, if you didn't know, not all Christians agree that December 25 is the most important date in early Jesus's life). So, yeah, even if you aren't Christian—even if you aren't religious at all—your phone still has you on the hook to remember when somebody else's god got born. Every. Single. Year.

▪ ▪ ▪

Confused? Overwhelmed? Don't worry—we'll come back to all of these concepts throughout the book. For now, here's what you need to know:

Religion is working all around you, all the time, whether you know it or not.

Religion is always, *always*, ALWAYS about power.

And religion is not even a little bit done with you.

So doesn't it seem like folks should pay more attention to religion and how it structures the world around us? And by "folks," we mean "you specifically, person currently holding this book," but also "everybody who lives in a world that is being shaped by religion even if they don't know it, which is to say, everybody?"

We sure think so. If you agree, turn the page.

CHAPTER 1

RELIGION IS (NOT) BASEBALL

*in which we use Red Sox Nation
to explain why religion is not a spectator sport*

I f religion is what people do, how exactly *do* people do religion? The whole premise of this book is asking you to pay attention to religion—but what are we asking you to look for?

Sometimes religion looks like whatever people who say they're doing religion are, you know, doing. But sometimes it's more complicated than that. Religion can happen in special ways in special places on special times of the day at special times of the year, but religion can also be ordinary, everyday, homey, routine. Religion is on our maps, on and in our bodies, and embedded in systems of power. We find religion all over the world today, but this wasn't always the case. With religion being so big and so amorphous, how can we even learn to look for it, much less think about it?

Batter up, friends. Hear that call? The time has come for us to pitch you an idea that at first might seem like a curveball: baseball's a really great way to start thinking about religion. (It's no closer, as you'll see, but a major league starter.)

This chapter takes you out to the ballgame and helps you watch religion at work in the world. And it's

1. providing you with a scouting report that will show you what to look for in your starting line-up—namely, *community*, *culture*, and *ritual*; and
2. putting *religious voluntarism* and *belief* on the DL, because religion is about so much more than that; and
3. coaching you through why *power* knocks baseball out of the religion park—because, sure, religion and the Boston Red Sox share a lot in common, but nobody is oppressing anybody on the basis of baseball (no matter what anybody says when the Yankees are in town.)

Time out, sports fans: We're using a playful metaphor throughout this chapter to introduce complicated theories. But religion does some really serious work in the world! Homes, lives, and countries are lost in the name of religion. People use religion to do some of the best and some of the worst things you can possibly imagine. No matter how you personally feel about religion, religion is shaping the world around you right this very minute—and it has been for centuries. So, regardless of our silliness, it's important that you know religion is not a game.

Got it?

Good.

Let's get back out there.

THERE'S NO "I" IN TEAM: RELIGION IS WHAT *PEOPLE* DO

Let's start with some warm-ups, champ. First up: religion is what *people* do, not just what one person does on their own. We're benching the "spiritual but not religious" folks for now; the highlights are that SBNR as a philosophy often ignores both its reductive assumptions about religion (the religion SBNR is not looks an awful lot like white mainstream Christianity) and its tendency to appropriate practices and materials outside their (often minoritized, frequently either Native or so-called Eastern) contexts. There are plenty of great books on the SBNR; this is not one of them. For the purposes of *this* book, "religion" is a collective noun.

Religion is what people do, and people learn to be people from other people. We pass those ways of being on to yet other people, often before they're even old enough to understand what we are passing them (or that they are people at all). Language, customs, social norms, ideas about selfhood, styles of dress—all of this comes from socialization and living in societies. Just like religion.

There is no religion without people, and there's no such thing as an inherently religious person. There is, with absolutely no apologies to Dean Hamer, no such thing as a "God gene," and no part of your brain is "naturally" religious. "Religion" only means what we—people—make it mean.

Religion is what we scholars call a "social construct," something that people (societies) make meaning of (construction). Race (chapter 3) and gender and sexuality (chapter 4) are also social constructs: they're meaning we make on, in, through, and about bodies for the purposes of telling ourselves which sorts of bodies we should value more and which bodies are, systemically speaking, disposable. Like all social constructs, religion is a way of not just identifying but *organizing* humans for the purposes of maintaining existing hierarchies.

We hope we pitched that one right over the plate, but it's okay if it was a swing and a miss for you. And if it was, don't worry, we'll come back to it a bunch. But before we slide into the next inning, it's important you see how much is riding on religion.

People use religion in all sorts of ways:

- as a way of marking themselves as good/moral people ("I'm religious")

- as a way of marking themselves as part of a group ("I'm Jewish," "I'm witchy")
- as an explanatory device in popular media ("Muslim terrorist" or "Christian extremist," though one of those shows up a *lot* more in headlines, and it's not the one you'd expect statistically)
- as a response to major life changes, crises, uncertainty ("no atheists in foxholes")
- as a strategy for claiming territory, resources, and lives (plenty of Jews and Muslims probably expected the Spanish Inquisition, but, alas . . .)
- as a strategy for resistance, survival, and belonging (unions, the civil rights movement, anti-war protests)
- as part of citizenship, statehood, asylum, medical care, and human rights (swearing in ceremonies, "so help you God" [whose God?] to testify in court)
- as a way of structuring and organizing time (yes! Even time itself is wrapped up in religion! We'll talk about this more in the homework chapter. For now, suffice it to say that if you've ever had a sewage flood in your basement on December 24, you know all too well that religion structures time. This happened to Ilyse, and religion—not *her* religion!—very much impeded her ability to find a plumber that day.)

When we say religion only means what people make it mean, we're saying there are as many ways of defining religion as there are ways of doing religion. Head coach (er, godfather and preeminent scholar of religious studies) J. Z. Smith taught us that "religion is not a native category." By this, he meant that religion isn't inherent or essential in and of itself. Religion is *not* a universal term; it does not come factory-installed on all individuals, all societies, all people. Religion is, rather, a descriptive category we apply to languages, beliefs, practices, rituals, clothing, philosophies, foodways, kinship networks, moral systems, and so much more.

Saying that nothing and no one are essentially religious might sound weird, wrong, or even offensive to you. So let's be clear: in saying that religion is descriptive, a social construct, we are *not* saying that religion is imaginary or fake. We're saying people mean a lot of different things when they say "religion," and as religious studies scholars—this means you too, sport—we have to pay attention to and take seriously all the different ways all the different kinds of people do all the different religions. In our expert opinion, people tend to use religion to create *culture* through *community* and *ritual*, and to cultivate and disrupt *power*. Sometimes those uses of religion are intentional and obvious; other times religion is harder to follow. But keep your eye on the ball and we'll talk you through it. Allow us, if you will, to take you out to the ball game.

FIRST AT BAT: CULTURE, COMMUNITY, AND RITUAL

If you've never lived in Boston, it might seem odd that two religious studies professors want to start a conversation about religion with the Red Sox. (Especially since only one of us is even a little bit sporty. Spoiler: it's Ilyse.) But if you've been in Boston between April to September—or, in a good year, October—this metaphor probably feels like a home run.

When Ilyse first moved to Boston in the mid-aughts, on weekends she was a frequent visitor to Haymarket, a chaotic and (most important for a grad student) affordable outdoor food market downtown. Now, Ilyse is a Jock™ from the part of New Jersey that claims to be New York City, and, as such, she owned a lot of Yankees paraphernalia. She also owns a lot of glorious but occasionally unruly curls. So, one unruly-curled summer day, on her way out the door to catch the T to Haymarket, she threw on a Yankees cap.

Strikes one, two, *and* three.

It's 8:30 a.m. on a Saturday. Orange line. The looks. The stares. The one dude in head-to-toe Sox gear yelling, "Oh for [redacted]'s sake, [redacted] no." Because Ilyse, unintentionally but unforgivably, had broken the first commandment of Boston: thou shalt not fly enemy colors. We'll remind you that this is a town where Megan heard fans shrieking "Yankees suck!" after the Patriots won the 2002 Super Bowl, a championship for a sport the Yankees do not play. Wearing Yankees gear on the T the summer after the Sox had reversed the curse? You're out. Ilyse had run afoul of *culture*.

When we say "culture," we mean "stuff made by humans who see themselves as a coherent group." Culture is a messy jumble of aesthetics, customs, language, institutions, art, literature, music, ways of organizing space and time, and (Megan's personal autistic least favorite) unspoken assumptions about how people should conduct themselves in a particular community's space and time. Even in one specific place, culture changes over time. But culture doesn't *feel* constructed. It feels natural, instinctual, the way things *should* be. Culture, in short, feels like home. Even when you don't feel at home in it.

Red Sox Nation will never feel like home to her, but grad-school Ilyse found herself in the thick of it. Whether or not she'd ever wanted to learn what a Big Papi is, Sox culture was right in her face—and possibly endangering her safety. Look, we cannot speak to the intentions of the [redacted] Red Sox fan, but men swearing at women in public ends badly for women all the time. So, when we say "socially constructed" doesn't mean "imaginary" or "fake," this is what we mean. Culture can seem silly, especially if you're not a part of it. Grown men getting mad at a stranger wearing a hat that represents other grown men whose employment requires them to hit balls with sticks definitely seems silly to us—but that doesn't mean this moment wasn't dangerous. That random men on public transportation would menace or even threaten Ilyse because of what she unthinkingly put on her head that morning seems almost unbelievable (but our hijabi and Sikh friends are for sure feeling this one). Culture has real material effects, and cultural competency can, in some instances, be a matter of personal safety or even survival.

Because here's the thing about culture: you can't ever entirely opt out. You can refuse to participate. Depending on your social position (education, job, wealth, proximity to power), you might have more or less space to resist or shift culture. You can evenly actively root against culture, as Ilyse unwittingly did all those weekends ago. But you can't ever get completely *outside* of the culture of the place and time in which you live. That's actually a rule of culture, as comedians and *Las Culturistas* podcasters Bowen Yang and Matt Rogers would say. Culture is not optional.

You've probably gathered by now that the Red Sox are a pretty big part of Boston's culture—which means whether you have never thought about sports or nurse a nearly twenty-year-old grudge because of Johnny Damon's epic betrayal of the city, it's nearly impossible to opt out of baseball in Boston. Boston baseball has its own special space: Fenway Park on Yawkey Way (now Jersey Street, just blocks from where Megan went to college). Baseball structures time in Boston, as any professor who's tried to schedule classes on opening day quickly learns. Baseball informs how and whether you can get into, out of, or around the city for roughly half the year. Baseball marks public spaces, even roadways (or it did until the 2004 World Series win made the "Reverse the Curse" graffiti on that Storrow Drive underpass redundant) and public notices (when the weather beacon atop the old John Hancock building flashes red it means bad weather—unless it's during Sox season, in which case flashing red means a home game has been postponed). Baseball players and fans infamously have their own rituals; players and fans don colorful outfits to signal their allegiance to the team. When the team wins or loses, much of the city experiences a shared public outburst of emotion. And, as Ilyse learned firsthand, profaning the rituals of Red Sox Nation carries dire consequences—which means baseball is also a way Bostonians determine who belongs in the city and who is unwelcome.

All of these qualities baseball shares with religion. Religion, like baseball, designates certain places, times, practices, people, and clothing as significant, set apart from the everyday. Religion, like baseball, marks boundaries—creating ways of distinguishing who belongs from who (like Ilyse in her cursed Yankees cap) does not or cannot. Because baseball, like religion, is about culture.

But let's stick with religion and baseball drawing and reinforcing lines between insiders and outsiders for a minute. Because religion, like baseball, is also about *community*. Sure, you can practice alone, but there's no game without a team. Red Sox Nation is literally a collection of fans. And when the team and the fans gather in the same place at the same time—for training, games, celebrations, defeats—that shared experience draws all those people closer together and provides a sense of identity and belonging, creating what sociologist of religion Emile Durkheim called "collective effervescence." It's that sensation of being part of something important. It feels like "you really just had to be there."

So, community is another way baseball works like religion. Of course you can believe or even practice on your own, but it's just not religion without other folks to learn from, to teach, to celebrate and mourn and try to make sense of the world with. Doing religion with other people—like being a Red Sox fan—is one way of creating and maintaining identity, a way to learn about ourselves and others. Doing religion together, like watching games or tracking stats or wearing your team's hat, fosters a sense of belonging. Like baseball, religion provides occasions and spaces to bring people together for a common purpose and a shared understanding of the world and our place in it. And like those Red Sox fans on the T, religion also draws lines between who's in—which is to say who's safe, who's included, who's protected—and who's out.

Communities often define themselves and their borders through *rituals*: often formalized actions and scripted words that create change, designate specific seasons and spaces as special, and sanctify treasured objects that do or mean more than they appear to. Rituals combine meanings and symbols and beliefs and commitments and teachings into a repeated and repeatable, often-but-not-always formalized series of actions and behaviors that matter to the participants and their community. Rituals tell us something important about the culture of participants. Rituals transform participants, bring communities together, draw boundaries between participants and outsiders. Rituals can be ways to access power and to disrupt power, build relationships or draw boundaries, create and contest value and meaning and authority.

Not all rituals are religious, of course! And not all religious practices are rituals. Ritual needn't be formal to be meaningful or worth paying attention to. Ritual can be laden with meaning and yet back of mind for individuals or even communities. Ritual at Fenway might include singing "Sweet Caroline" during the eighth inning or trying to graffiti Pesky's Pole, or—to Ilyse's ongoing chagrin—screaming "Yankees suck" at any time, against any opponent. (Megan would like to point out that the suckage of the Yankees is ontological rather than statistical.) Knowing when and how to clap, sing, or scream "Yankees suck"? Those kinds of rituals create and reinforce culture, build and solidify community—regardless of how any one individual who happens to be *in* Boston on any given day personally feels about the sport of baseball or the local team itself.

FOUL BALLS: BELIEF ONLY GETS A PIECE OF IT

When you root, root, root for the home team, that's a smart choice—certainly it will keep the home fans in line, not causing a ruckus for you or yours. But choosing to root for the home team underlines a really key idea in religion. An idea that, frankly, dominates how wrongly we think about religion.

Americans in particular often think of being religious as a set of choices, kind of like picking a team cap to wear, but instead of that "NY" or "LA" or, fine, that "B" emblem, you're basically picking where you want to go after you die. We talk about religion as if you can choose to do it or not to do it—but either way, it's your choice, right?

Not so much, really, no. Turns out it's not so simple. If you, say, grow up in a family of Sox fans, you don't *have* to be one, too, but the likelihood of rooting for the Chicago Cubs is slimmer. Where and when we're born and to whom determines the religious options available to us. This means that religious belonging (and maybe fandom) isn't *entirely* voluntary.

We can choose whether we personally want to do religion or not, and even within religions we can often choose how to participate, what rituals to engage in, which particular communities to cultivate. But religion is bigger than personal choice. Religion impacts and is itself a system. So, in countries shaped by religion—which is all of them, though often in very different ways—we can't wash our hands of religion altogether. You cannot take off your team's cap.

Religious voluntarism—the idea that we *choose* what to believe and what community to belong to or leave entirely—assumes white Christianity and specifically white Protestantism. What Americans consider "good" or "acceptable" religion is usually private, individual, and opt-in. This is a very white Western Protestant understanding of religion, as Winnifred Sullivan compellingly argues in her killjoy classic *The Impossibility of Religious Freedom* (2005). And that Protestant understanding of religion asserts that it is and should be absorbed into how we think about everyday life, across religions, institutions, and settings.

The religion that's *bad* is everything else: communal religion, collective religion, cultural religion, religions that are tied to ethnicities and often races, religions that have their own languages. *Religions that you cannot opt out of without opting out of, well, everything else in our* *society*. This is one of the ways the world religions paradigm sorted and categorized religions: Western Euro-American empires favored religious traditions they perceived as most similar to Protestant Christianity and policed and penalized other "less civilized" traditions.[*] Further away from those Western Christian norms? Less power, less prestige, less validity—more oppression, persecution, troubles. (We spend all of chapter 2 on these very big, very crucial topics, but a little taste never hurt anyone, right?)

In short, then: the idea of religious voluntarism assumes *belief* defines religious belonging, and we are trying to say that belief is a foul ball—it gets a piece of what religion is, but does not count as a hit. Belief assumes that religion is *only* or *mostly* a matter of an individual's choice in their innermost thoughts and feelings. Belief also assumes, bluntly, that individuals can choose to *be* a Christian (hence all the street preachers trying to get us all to be exactly that). Except *being* a Jewish, Muslim, Hindu, Sikh, or Native practitioner has everything to do with communities, identities, practices, sometimes even heredity. And you often cannot opt out of those things, even if you want to.

Some topics to keep your eyes on as this book unfolds, all of which trouble the centrality of belief and religious voluntarism: An atheist Jew who does not believe nor practice Judaism can still experience antisemitism. A Sikh can experience Islamophobia because his turban is read in particular (and particularly troubling) ways. A man named Ahmed who claims no religion for himself can still be profiled by the TSA under suspicion of Islamic terrorism. None of these has to do with belief.

This is because religion doesn't *have* to be about belief! And religion *isn't* about belief for a lot of practitioners and communities. For a

---

[*] The world religions paradigm is an assumption about religion's universality. Since the beginning of modernity (1500s on), Western Euro-American imperialism uses this idea to justify and enforce many policies, rules, regulations, and stereotypes. This paradigm is the subject of chapter 2.

lot of religious communities—Jews and Muslims and Hindus, for starters—being religious is less about *thinking* or *believing* the right things
about the divine, and more about *doing* what's necessary to be in right
relationship with the divine, one's community, and oneself. For these
practitioners, it's more important to cultivate correct actions, observe
the right practices, and comport one's body in proper ways than to
have faith in God/s. What's more, doubt and questioning are central
to Judaism (which makes Ilyse an *exemplary* Jew, for the record). One
needn't believe in God to be Jewish.

For that matter, not all religions have deities! Jainism doesn't have
deities! Neither do many forms of Buddhism or Daoism! Confucianism
doesn't! (We also only think about Confucianism as a religion because
of some Western European Christian colonial nonsense, about which
more in chapter 2.) And for a lot of polytheists, belief is a nonstarter
and a borderline offensive way to think or talk about the Divine. Gods
and goddesses don't need us to believe in them; they just *are*. Using
religion and belief interchangeably reinforces a very specific and very
Christian way of thinking about religion. Which is why we'd love for
folks to stop using the two terms interchangeably.

And what's more, even if you *do* participate in religious rituals—
rituals that *mean* something—ritual is not just acting out beliefs. You
don't have to be a Red Sox fan to sing "Sweet Caroline" in the eighth,
because you don't necessarily have to believe in anything to participate
in a ritual. Just singing "Sweet Caroline" doesn't immediately naturalize
you into Red Sox nation. Ilyse has done this, without rooting for the
Sox, without seeing herself as a permanent or stable part of the community, without being clocked as a Yankees fan, and still doesn't see
why Boston thinks it's so great. (Then again, she cares way more about
things like batting averages and games won than Megan does.) Some
find that participating in rituals with community fosters and strength-
ens their convictions in that community's worldview; others participate
in rituals despite skepticism, apathy, or even disbelief. Sometimes we

go to a game, or go to shul, out of obligation or habit or just not having other plans that day or to make our family or community happy.

So, when it comes to religion or baseball, belief doesn't cover the whole field. Belief isn't uniform or consistent even within a single religious tradition; even people who share the same beliefs might act out those beliefs differently. (In the same way that there's a vast difference between, say, season-ticket holders and folks who catch a game on TV every once in a while.) Sure, belief and opting in can be *part* of religion or baseball—but it only ever gets a piece of the ball. It's never going to be a hit.

A foul ball doesn't get the batter on base, and belief doesn't get us that close to understanding religion—what people do *with* and *about* religion. We cannot ascertain what people *truly* believe; people act in ways that contradict what they say their beliefs are all the time. Perhaps more importantly, though, belief tells us very little about what matters most to understanding baseball or religion: power.

YOU'RE OUTTA HERE: RELIGION IS NOT BELIEF, ACTUALLY

This is where our metaphor might need a relief pitcher, because baseball is not actually religion. Baseball doesn't provide an explanation for how all humans or even just all Bostonians came to be or tell Red Sox fans how to behave if they want their consciousness to continue after their bodies have stopped working. Both are key aspects of many major religious traditions. But the real reason we're benching this metaphor is because baseball doesn't help us think about how power works through systems.

It's not that the Red Sox aren't powerful. Boston baseball culture controls traffic, sets the tone for postgame train rides, predicts law enforcement coverage throughout the city, shifts business practices and school calendars, shapes interpersonal interactions (on public transit and elsewhere), and sometimes even influences individuals' and groups' safety, as Ilyse learned on the train that day.

We're not going to lie: that interaction was scary for Ilyse and could have ended very badly. But to avoid that situation in the future, Ilyse can choose not to wear a Yankees hat in Boston. (She shouldn't have to, because what people put on their bodies is nobody's goddamn business as long as it isn't literal hate speech; get over yourself, Boston.) Other identities can't be discarded so easily. Ilyse can take off her Yankees hat in a way that she cannot shake her Jewish identity. If Ilyse was assaulted or harassed for wearing a Yankees hat, the Boston police could not and would not file that as a hate crime. If Ilyse was assaulted or harassed for being Jewish, however, there are protections in place for that identity.

This distinction matters because religion—as identities, as communities, as worldviews—shapes our systems and affects us collectively. An individual's safety may be at risk due to another individual's (deranged) fandom: Boston fans, bless them, have been known to riot when they win *and* when they lose. That is not the same as the mayor of Boston being able to pass ordinances about only wearing Sox gear, or barring Yankees fans from public offices, or disallowing the broadcast of Yankees games on radio. Compare this to the ways that, for example, the Canadian state of Quebec passed Bill 21, legislation barring people who wear religious garb to hold particular public positions of authority, including schoolteachers; the law tacitly targets Muslim women who cover, Sikh men who don turbans, and, to a lesser degree, observant Jewish men, while leaving all manner of Christians unscathed, under the guise of separation of church and state. Laws like this target vulnerable religious minorities while reinforcing the normality, the necessity of Christian traditions. State-regulated religious norms (like the Quebec bill) have real-world consequences in ways that social norms (about baseball hats or anything else people do together) just don't.

As we keep telling you, power is really what we want you to focus on when you're thinking about religion. How do institutions and organizations not only reflect social biases but also preserve and protect the privileges and resources at the top of social hierarchies? How do they determine control, influence, authority, leverage, or access to resources in a system or systems? Power flows through systems, including religious ones.

If we're taking religion seriously—we are and hope you will too—we cannot ignore how systems use, codify, protect, and exploit religion. Religion is a system of power *and* religion is part of structural power systems, as we'll see shortly when we explore the world religions paradigm. Systemic and structural power is what matters when we are thinking about religion. Power shapes our everyday lives. Power is what makes religion both dangerous and liberatory.

▪   ▪   ▪

While it strikes out as a perfect metaphor, baseball is still a fun way to start thinking critically about religion. For fans, watching a game can feel like being part of something, maybe even a big something (community). For Boston fans, stadiums like Fenway are more than just some grass and dirt (culture). There is a *feeling* of watching a game live: excitement, togetherness, mostly everyone rooting for the same thing, folks singing the same chants, moving their bodies in the same way (ritual).

But baseball doesn't shape systems to the same extent and with the same persistence religion does (power). In the next chapter, we'll push you to think more about how religion came to be so tangled up in systems like empires and—believe it or not!—maps.

▪ ▪ ▪ ▪ ▪ ▪ ▪ ▪ ▪ ▪

RELIGION ALL-STAR STARTING LINEUP

(P) Clifford Geertz on culture

(C) Talal Asad on secularism

(SS) Émile Durkheim on community

(1B) Catherine Bell on ritual

(2B) Caroline Walker Bynum on gender

(3B) Grace Janzen on presence

(LF) Yvonne Chireau on race

(CF) Tomoko Masuzawa on world religions

(RF) James Baldwin on power

(DH) Saba Mahmood on belief

(M) J. Z. Smith

FURTHER READING

Malory Nye, *Religion: The Basics* (London: Routledge, 2003)

Raquel Romberg, *Witchcraft and Welfare: Spiritual Capital and the Business of Magic in Modern Puerto Rico* (Austin: University of Texas Press, 2004)

Winnifred Fallers Sullivan, *The Impossibility of Religious Freedom: New Edition* (Princeton, NJ: Princeton University Press, 2018)

FURTHER LISTENING ON KEEPING IT 101

(E101) "What the Heck Is Religion, and What the Heck Is This Podcast?"

(E105) "What Does It Mean to be 'Religious'?"

(E201) "Race, Gender, and Sexuality: What's Religion Got to Do with 'Em?"

(E512) "INCORRECT: Sports"

CHAPTER 2

RELIGION IS GLOBAL

*in which we reveal the creation of "religion"
through the cunning use of maps*

In the last chapter, we played around with the idea that religion is a lot like baseball. But that doesn't mean religion is a game! There are real-world stakes to this idea, and real-world consequences to doing it in ways those in power find unpalatable. It might seem unbelievable that religion, something so many of us perceive as deeply personal, could have such a global impact. But the concept of religion—and especially the idea that religion is something all humans have done throughout all times and all places, otherwise known as the "world religions paradigm"—has literally made and remade countries, shaping how we think about ourselves and others (even if we ourselves are not religious).

But wait, *isn't* religion universal? Doesn't it show up always and everywhere?

Sorry to give you the nerd answer, friends, but, kind of? Sort of? It's complicated? Also nope.

Let's get into it.

■   ■   ■

What comes to mind when you hear the phrase "world religions"? Maybe you took a world religions class in high school or college. (Megan has taught a LOT of these.) Maybe you've visited your favorite independent bookseller and wondered why books about religion are separated into Eastern Religions and Western Religions. (Ilyse has received a lot of text messages from Megan that basically boil down to "They put Islam under Eastern Religions again. I am finding the manager.") Maybe you've listened to a podcast or two about what religion looks like all over the world. (Oh, hey, *Keeping It 101* has a whole award-winning season on that!) Maybe you've seen, or even own, one of those bumper stickers urging us all to *coexist*, where the letters are made of symbols that represent different religious traditions. If so, this chapter is for you.

World religions often makes people think of the so-called Big Five: Christianity, Judaism, Islam, Hinduism, and Buddhism. If you're really interested in religion—and we hope you are, since you're reading this book and all—maybe you also know something about Sikhi or Zoroastrianism, or, heck, even some new religious movements. "World religions" is one of those phrases that sound really inclusive, like "COEXIST" or "Love Is Love." World religions classes and textbooks usually offer a tasting menu of traditions, letting consumers sample cultures and practices different from their own. The basic premise of world religions is most often "Sure, maybe we have different ways of seeing the world but also we're all pretty much the same. Can't we all just be cool and groovy to each other like in *Toy Story 3*?" "World religions" sounds, well, *nice*.

But, like many things created by white people claiming to speak for the whole of humanity, "world religions" is not at all nice. "World religions" tells us that religion exists and has existed in all times and all places (it has not). "World religions" divides traditions, cultures, even whole populations, into "major" and "minor" religious traditions, which has material consequences (particularly for those of us who find ourselves on the "minor" side of that particular equation). "World religions" conceals violent imperial histories and presents, because "religion" as we now understand it got its start in the service of empire. In fact: world religions *made* borders—and those borders are still making religious and political realities all over the world today.

This chapter will walk you through how we came to identify certain practices, spaces, texts, and ways of being as religious. Spoilers: "religion" is newer, messier, and more violent than you probably know, and "world religions" is a framework that tells us a lot about that very modern, very violent mess.

Please note: When we say that religion is new, messy, and violent, this does *not* mean that religion itself is inherently violent. Religion isn't inherently anything. As we discussed in the last chapter, religion is what people do—and some people do messy and violent things with religion. But now we're pushing you to look a little closer at how we learned to call a specific part of human experience "religion." Part of thinking critically about religion is recognizing that the history of religion and the deployment of the concept *is* incontrovertibly violent and indisputably connected to the history of Western imperialism. Which is what this chapter is about.

"World religions"—the phrase, the paradigm, the whole system that rests on its assumptions (and its cousin-terms "major" and "minor" religions)—has done and continues to do some real harm in the world. Empires use religion to draw and redraw physical and political borders, which can render people vulnerable and displace whole populations. Nation-states and international organizations use religion to determine who is worthy of aid, who deserves asylum, whose humanity is worth defending.

But "world religions" also does more intimate harm. "World religions" helps determine whether you have to—or are even allowed to—take a day off to celebrate your holiday, whether you can easily find food that meets your dietary requirements, whether people who share your background are also serving in government positions. In the United States, "world religions" informs if and how the First Amendment protects your community and if hate crimes against your community can be recognized as such under law. On a global scale, "world religions" influences textbooks, public celebrations, national identity, and international aid—if your religious community's rituals, dress, foodways, and texts get included or if you and your people drop out of the story altogether.

In this chapter, we're telling you "world religions" is a problem because

- Western European empires created the concept of religion (pretty recently, as it turns out)
- Western European empires used religion and "world religions" to divide and conquer the world—religion literally creates borders and nations

but also

- peoples all over the world use religion to survive, disrupt, and resist empire (with mixed results) in the wake of colonialism and imperialism

Thinking critically about world religions matters because the paradigm does material harm, especially in systems created and maintained through white European Christian imperial force. "World religions" is a big freaking problem! But thinking critically about world religions also matters because minoritized people use "religion" to resist, survive, and thrive. Which is why we're not arguing, as plenty of others have, to get rid of world religions altogether.

We really don't want folks to stop saying "world religions," or stop teaching students about other people's cultures and traditions, or deny that people meaningfully connect to the -ism assigned to them in the world religions paradigm. Two things can be and are true: the world religions paradigm has fundamentally altered the world, often through force, and people can work within that hegemonic system toward their own survival and flourishing. Our goal here is to work toward doing better—because, as acclaimed writer and civil rights activist James Baldwin teaches us again and again, systems are made by people. "One is not obliged to be at the mercy of the institution. You made it and you can unmake it," Baldwin told a UMass Amherst student in 1984, in a lecture that was later published under the title "Blacks and Jews." "Every system, social system, because it involves human beings in order to be made useful, has to be attacked and endlessly changed." With Baldwin, we want to insist that systems made by people can be remade—better, more equitable, more just—by people, too.

RELIGION? I DON'T KNOW HER

As you already know, nerds: religion is what people do. The previous chapter offered you a set of tools for thinking about religion, so you also know that "religion" is shorthand for a complex cluster of human behaviors, habits, structures, systems, and ways of seeing the world and our place in it. We told you that thinking about religion means paying attention to culture, community, ritual, power, and presence. For some religious folks—mostly but not exclusively Christians—belief is very important. But for many others, being religious is much more about how they are in the world on a day-to-day basis. And, as we've discussed, people act in ways that contradict what they believe (or say they do) all the time.

But if you've taken a class or listened to a podcast or watched a documentary series on world religions, you might have noticed that they tend to focus on the core beliefs of specific religious traditions, as well as a central sacred text, a singular (often male) founder, special buildings used for prayers or ceremonies, and maybe special dress or customs. What's the big deal about belief? Why do we assume all religions would be grounded in belief? Heck, why do we even think "religion" is something we can find all over the world?

Pro tip: the answer to this and just about every question in this chapter (and, frankly, this book and possibly just in life?) is white European Christian imperialism.

It might seem odd to hear that religion hasn't existed in all times and all places. What about the ancient Greeks or Hindus? Those guys were lousy with deities! Weren't the Egyptian pharaohs considered divine? Isn't some of the earliest writing we have about religion?!

We hate to do the professor thing at you, but: yes and no. Yes, humans have probably always told stories about how things came to be the way they are, marked seasons and life stages, formed relationships with more- or other-than-humans, observed certain customs about the beginning and end of life, and a thousand other qualities we now bundle into "religion."

Before Western European imperial expansion, people the world over understood themselves in ways that *might* look and sound like what we think of as religion, or culture, or just living. Many groups we now think of as religious—like Jews or Muslims or Sikhs or Parsis—pre-date the modern concept of religion. Some groups we now think of as religious existed for millennia before "religion": they had names for themselves, coherent group identities, rituals and celebrations and languages and art and spaces they marked as important, significant, out of the ordinary. But those people didn't use this really specific European word, "religion," to describe members of their group or members of other peoples' groups.

Often—as J. Z. Smith has famously argued—these people didn't have a local concept that maps onto the European concept of religion, either. Admittedly, "religion" has cognate terms in other places all over the world (like the Islamic concept of *din*, for example). And these terms share some common characteristics with religion—but they were deployed differently in different contexts. What we now call "religion" is a system of power that's implemented in really specific ways in a very specific historical and geographical context.

Religion as we think of it today doesn't emerge, as best we can tell, until about the seventeenth century. And it specifically emerges out of—you guessed it!—white European Christian imperialism.

Picture it: University of Wittenberg, Germany, 1517. A priest and professor of moral theology has had it, *officially*, with the Roman Catholic Church. He posts a long list of grievances—ninety-five grievances, to be exact—on the door of a local church. By the time the dust settles, he's accidentally created a whole new way to be Christian.

Martin Luther was, of course, not the first person to suggest that the Roman Catholic Church was getting it wrong, especially when it came to people's relationship to the divine . . . and the Church's relationship to people's money. But for the most part, folks who openly defied the Church didn't survive long enough to do much after that. The Roman Catholic Church controlled the entirety of Western Europe for centuries. There was no separation of government from obligations to the church, which shaped everything from gender roles to economies to foodways to measuring time. (In 1582, Pope Gregory XIII created the calendar we still use today—we'll come back to Christian supremacy and calendars in the homework.) Religion wasn't part of who an individual person was: the practices, worldviews, and systems we'd now identify as religious were the whole dang show.

Until Luther's attempt to reform his church of ordination transformed, instead, into the establishment of a separate sect altogether—a sect that grew so much in size and influence that heads of European kingdoms began to embrace it. Those self-proclaimed Protestants found themselves at odds with kingdoms ruled by Catholic monarchs, which escalated into the Wars of Religion, spanning from the early sixteenth to early eighteenth centuries across Western Europe. In their wake would emerge important ways of reordering the world: concepts like science (including its genocidal offspring, race), universities, nations (and their murderous spouse, borders, and more on that in the next section), imperialism, and, that's right, religion.

It is hard to overstate just how much this period, which historians call "modernity," fundamentally reshapes the entire world, not just Europe. Europe, of course, doesn't invent everything itself: that is a racist lie that Europe taught the globe. It can *seem* like Europe is the be-all and end-all of modernity, especially when we're spending so much time talking about how European modernity fundamentally reshaped the rest of the world. *Mais non!* Europe extracted much of its modern inspiration from global reservoirs, built on them, and then imagined itself as the most important, most intelligent, most blessed entity ever to grace the globe. So, naturally, Europe needed—nay, was honor-bound—to impose its understanding of itself and Others throughout the rest of the world.

Take, for example, science. While Europe plodded through its Dark Ages (which scholars have recently argued were maybe not so dark after all), knowledge production we now call "science" was booming throughout the Middle East and Southwest, Central, and South Asia. While even the most affluent white Christian Europeans struggled to literally figure their shit out (don't get Ilyse started on historical potties), Muslim empires sponsored and benefited from all manner of math, astronomy, physics, philosophical, and linguistic sciences. When Europe got modern, those earlier, Muslim-led discoveries benefited and informed Western European Christian science.

At which point Western European Christian scientists used this accumulated global way of knowing to prove that everyone who was *not* a white Western European Christian was inherently, essentially, *scientifically* inferior. This is where and when the concept of race emerges; we'll come back to this in the next chapter. For now . . .

Europe, and we cannot stress this enough, did not invent science. Nor did European scientific innovation develop solely out of Western European Christian thought. When we speak of modernity, we're referring to the historical period in which white Western European Christians borrowed, adapted, and instrumentalized global ways of knowing to support and justify their imperial agenda. Science and schools and economic systems and laws and empires and even groups we'd now call religions absolutely existed before modernity! But the world's understanding of these institutions—and more importantly, the Western European imperial enforcement of uniformity, consistency, and globalism among and throughout these institutions—is a thoroughly modern one.

That's why we're saying that religion—the idea that all people everywhere *have* religion—a term that here means ideologies, rituals, customs, cultures, languages, even ethnicities and races—is a modern concept. Religion emerges in what's called the modern era in Western European history (beginning in the early sixteenth century). And religion emerges in the modern era specifically as a product of European imperialism and Western Christian domination, when countries like Spain and Portugal, and later England and France, began conquering the world on the premise that *uncivilized people* needed *Christianity* and *Christian civilization* in order to be *people* at all. This is why when we talk about religion we are always also talking about communities and cultures shaped by European colonialism and imperialism.

We promise this isn't just egghead semantics. Imposing religion meant classifying some things as "religion" and other things as not for the purposes of identifying whose lives matter and whose are disposable. European Christian empires used those systems of power— colonialism and imperialism, of which religion is indelibly a part—to expand their reach and extract resources, including human beings, across the globe. That's what we mean when we say "religion," as a concept, grows out of white European Christian supremacy. And because religion grows out of white European Christian supremacy, religion is never separate from the white European Christian practices of colonialism, imperialism, and orientalism.

Before we get to what all of this has to do with "world religions," let's be sure we're all on the same page about these terms. In *Religion, Science, and Empire* (2012), historian Peter Gottschalk defines colonialism as "the process through which a group overtakes another, usually in a way that is tied to lands, by way of force, extraction of resources, and other forms of domination, with the express purpose of economic benefit." Imperialism usually refers to the enforcement of *political* control over and above or in addition to economic gain or control. Western European nations justified colonialism and imperialism in large part *through* religion, insisting that their brand of Christian civilization would improve—indeed, save—those peoples whose lands they claimed, resources they stole, lives they exploited and ended.

No, seriously. Just check out this excerpt from *Inter Caetera*, the document in which Pope Alexander VI gave the entire "uncivilized" world to Spain and Portugal in 1493. This papal imperative would come to be known as the "Doctrine of Discovery"; we'll come back to it in chapter 3. Here goes:

> Wherefore, as becomes Catholic kings and princes, after earnest consideration of all matters, especially of the rise and spread of the Catholic faith, as was the fashion of your ancestors, kings of renowned memory, you have purposed with the favor of divine clemency to bring under your sway the said mainlands and islands with their residents and inhabitants and to bring them to the Catholic faith. Hence, heartily commending in the Lord this your holy and praiseworthy purpose, and desirous that it be duly accomplished, and that the name of our Savior be carried into those regions, we exhort you very earnestly in the Lord and by

your reception of holy baptism, whereby you are bound to our apostolic commands, and by the bowels of the mercy of our Lord Jesus Christ, enjoy strictly, that inasmuch as with eager zeal for the true faith you design to equip and despatch this expedition, you purpose also, as is your duty, to lead the peoples dwelling in those islands and countries to embrace the Christian religion. . . .

Moreover we command you in virtue of holy obedience that, employing all due diligence in the premises, as you also promise—nor do we doubt your compliance therein in accordance with your loyalty and royal greatness of spirit—you should appoint to the aforesaid mainlands and islands worthy, God-fearing, learned, skilled, and experienced men, in order to instruct the aforesaid inhabitants and residents in the Catholic faith and train them in good morals. . . . We trust in Him from whom empires and governments and all good things proceed, that, should you, with the Lord's guidance, pursue this holy and praiseworthy undertaking, in a short while your hardships and endeavors will attain the most felicitious result, to the happiness and glory of all Christendom.

Told you so. In fact, the word "religion" itself comes from the Latin, *religio*. "Religion" was rooted in particular Christian practice and later expanded into Christian-dominated places to *describe* people and ways of life that Christians encountered, notably during and as part of imperial expansion. This is why scholars like Junaid Rana argue that the very concept of religion, especially as it is deployed in statecraft, is inherently antisemitic and Islamophobic. Part of the work of religion is dividing the world into worse and better, east and west, barbaric and civilized, violent and restrained, ignorant and educated, antiquated and modern. Jews and Muslims tended to find themselves on the sinister side of that equation, since the folks doing those calculations (i.e., white European Christians) were also the ones equating white European Christianity with modernity, education, and civilization. This all added up to what Palestinian scholar-activist Edward Said dubbed "orientalism."

Orientalism helps explain why we think about the world as "the East" and "the West," even though we famously live on a ball. In his paradigm-shifting book *Orientalism* (1978), Said argues that the West *understands* itself as the West—a white, intellectual, logical, masculine, Christian group of (rightful) global leaders—only by contrasting itself with the East. Using historical documents and literature, Said explained that all the things that come to mind when you imagine the East, all the carpets, the snake charmers, the domed architecture, the street bazaars, the flowing clothes, the turbans, the ladies in harems, the sumptuous and oversaturated colors: all of that is a product of imperialism and colonialism. At the same time, orientalism helped drive the European notion that the East *demanded* dominating, colonizing, *civilizing*: that the theft of Eastern resources and the exploitation of Eastern humans was for the good of all. And religion became the vehicle of that mission to civilize.

Religion is, at its heart, a measure of how close to or far from another tradition or culture is to white European Christianity. Religion got and gets used to make race, build empires, and define borders—all in service of establishing and upholding white European Christian dominion the world over. Religion is not a neutral metric through which to observe the world. It is a hierarchy that places white European Christianity at the top of the global org chart and ranks every other way of being in the world, to greater or lesser extents, as less-than. And that's where "world religions" comes in.

WHOSE EMPIRE IS IT ANYWAY?

The "world religions" paradigm is a way of describing the relationship between white European Christian empires and the peoples they sought to commodify and exploit. "World religions" has historically divided peoples and practices all over the globe into "major" and "minor" religions—major religions being the aforementioned "Big Five," to which we'll return in a minute, and minor religions being everyone else.

But, wait, we hear you saying. What does all this historical gobbledygook have to do with who makes the cut for the COEXIST bumper sticker?

It's empire all the way down, friends. We're paraphrasing here, but Said said that empire moved in two waves: the guys with guns and the guys with pens. First the guys with guns terrorize the would-be subjects of the empire, and then the guys with pens start making systems, describing the terrorized and newly colonized people back to themselves in ways that make their colonization, degradation, and dehumanization not only inevitable, but salutary. White Christian European empires told everybody else that they *had* to be colonized for their own good. Those guys with pens went on to create histories and laws and systems and schools that presented white European Christianity as the best, the most scientifically advanced, the most racially superior, the most philosophically sophisticated civilization ever to grace the earth. And then they wrote down rules so that following all this was mandatory.

Before we move on, let's be clear. We are in no way suggesting that white European Christians invented thinking they were god/s' gift to the world (Babylonians, anybody?) or even that they were the first group we'd now think of as religious to tell the rest of the world that the Divine likes them best. In medieval Muslim kingdoms, there would often be theological debates held between Jews, Muslims, and Christians about which was the superior tradition and—as the stories go—the winners were usually Muslim. Jews received so-so silver in this competition, while Christians take shameful bronze nearly every time (because how can monotheism also be a trinity? Medieval Muslims begged their Christian neighbors to make it make sense). Jewish records also show theologians and philosophers and rabbis and leaders proclaiming both their righteousness and their inherently better religion over and above Christians and Muslims. Arguments about whom the universe favors and how best to live are as old as humanity. But using religion as a concept and world religions as a paradigm to argue for an empire's economic, legal, racial, scientific, philosophical, and moral superiority over the rest of the world? That's a relatively new strategy, and unique to European Christians in the process of teaching themselves they were white (and, more damningly, that everyone else was not—more on the construction of race and religion in the next chapter).

So, once more with feeling: religion is a metric that measures all other ways of being in the world against white European Christianity and finds them wanting. But that doesn't mean that white European empires treated all ways of being religious the same. Groups that have a central sacred text; a single (often male) founder; distinct ways of dressing, eating, and acting; specific locations to interact with other- or more-than-humans; an appeal to universality (that is, one needn't be born into the religion); a specific house of worship; a traceable history—those groups now get called "religions."

The religions on that Big Five list we keep talking about all share these characteristics, to a greater or lesser extent. But that doesn't mean the list is simple or logical or even follows its own rules. "Major religions" includes Buddhism, which not all practitioners think of as a religion at all, and Hinduism, which for most of the history of the world would have been thousands of related but distinct practices and communities. The list includes Judaism, a numerical minority among groups we now call "religions," but not Sikhi, numerically the fifth largest religion in the world.

Let's talk about Sikhi (or Sikhism, as the colonizers would say) for a second. Because Sikhi is not a major religion in the world religions paradigm. But Sikhi has a single male founder and a traceable history: Guru Nanak revealed Sikhi in contemporary Punjab, a region of South Asia. Sikhi has houses of worship, gurdwaras; a central sacred text, the Guru Granth Sahib; and practices that mark them as a distinct religious community, including uncut hair and the turbans many Sikhs wear. Sikhi accepts converts. It checks all the "world religions" boxes. But world religions textbooks regularly omit or minimize Sikhi. You won't clock it on COEXIST.

This isn't to say that being on the major religions list is necessarily good news, either. Judaism and Islam being included tells us a lot about religion being unfavorably compared to Christianity. Being a major religion hasn't protected Jews from historic suppression as a religion or historic persecution as a people. Judaism makes the list because the makers of that list—the guys with pens—saw Judaism as a stepping stone toward the evolutionary superiority of Christianity. Likewise, Islam makes the list because the guys with the pens saw Muslims as a, if not *the*, primary threat to (European) Christian imperial domination.

Where did European monarchs get the idea that the world was theirs to define, divide, and conquer? Why, from the Church, of course—specifically the Roman Catholic Church and its now-notorious, only recently (as in March 2023) rescinded Doctrine of Discovery.

The Doctrine of Discovery, of which you read an excerpt just a few pages ago, is a set of papal bulls and international and domestic laws and policies that effectively grant European Christian empires dominion over any territory (and people) not previously dibsed by another European Christian empire. In the next chapter we'll talk more how about the Doctrine of Discovery and settler colonialism ravaged the Americas, but the short version is that this doctrine made European colonial and imperial expansion across the globe legal, moral, and necessary—rendering the territory, resources, bodies, and lives of the people in those "discovered" lands forfeit, and not just allowing but often encouraging missionaries to do unspeakable things in service of Christianizing conquered lands. From the sixteenth century until the twenty-first, the official position of the Roman Catholic Church was that not-white not-European not-Christians deserved and should expect—indeed, *be grateful for*—enslavement, rape, murder, and forced conversion.

Armies can get the enslavement, torture, rape, murder, and destruction started. But to really extract resources and maintain lasting dominance over a region, you need people to run the place. You need scholars. Administrators. Tax collectors. Law enforcement. Teachers, too. That's right: the guys with pens.

The pen isn't mightier than the sword in a duel, but pens sure do get the job done when it comes to creating and enforcing systems. Those guys use their pens to collect, make meaning of, and distribute information about colonized peoples to administrators, nobles, church councils, and parliaments. This information gathering isn't just an intellectual exercise; it's a technology of domination.

We know that Columbus sailed the ocean blue in 1492, but colonialism never stops with a Columbus (or Pizarro, or Cook, or whoever—insert the name of your least fave harbinger of genocide here). Empires run on information, and demographics (among other sets of knowledge) play a key role in the imperial apparatus. The guys with pens were an integral part of any boots-on-the-ground imperial invasion. These seemingly harmless nerds wanted to know who the empire was acquiring and how their (wrong, savage, barbaric) beliefs and practices compared to white European Christian norms.

So it makes sense that in the early- and mid-1500s we see documents, treatises, and books about the religions of others making their way back to the seat of European empires. At first glance, these publications appear journalistic: they describe what is happening and how the local culture or society understands it. They're written in a neutral tone. But the work that these texts do is far from neutral. The guys with pens classified, categorized, and compared colonized peoples and practices more or less favorably—more civilized, more advanced, more *human*—according to how closely those people and practices resembled white European Christianity. So it should come as no surprise that Islam, imagined as the antithesis to Christianity, fared particularly poorly in these reports.

Islam gets its start on the same peninsula as Judaism and Christianity, but you won't find Islam in the Western Religions section of most bookstores or among the classes taught in Western Religion curricula. This is orientalism in action: the West imagining itself as fundamentally different from and better than the East, Christianity imagining itself as fundamentally different from and better than Islam. If Christianity is a Western religion—advanced, rational, scientific, superior—then Islam must be an Eastern religion. In the world religions paradigm created by those guys with the pens, Eastern religions are excessive, violent, static, undisciplined, ruled by base urges rather than impartial logic. (Because, as we know, founder of the Anglican Church Henry VIII, for example, never indulged an urge.)

Animus among Christians and Muslims—like animus among Christians and other kinds of Christians—obviously pre-dates the invention of world religions, as famed historian of religion Tomoko Masuzawa calls it. But systems that characterize Islam as *incompatible with, a threat to, an abomination compared* with Western civilization are modern inventions directly tied to the invention of religion. Islam plays Christianity's foil in the global theater of European colonial and imperial expansion into Africa and Asia, the largest continents on Earth. The guys with pens (yes, them again) reported that Muslims could never truly become good subjects of empire and urged imperial forces to treat Muslims as suspicious and unruly: fundamentally, essentially ungovernable. And religion lay at the heart of those policy recommendations, because the world religions paradigm imagined Islam as everything Christianity wasn't, and therefore everything the West could not, must not, tolerate.

The next time you hear someone refer to the "Muslim world," pause and remember this chapter, because you just heard the world religions paradigm at work. In this worldview, *only* Europe and the northern parts of North America have civilization, which is to say the correct religion, which is to say Christianity. Everybody else—originally the East; presumably the global South now, which confusingly includes Mexico, a country in North America—does not, or didn't until contact with white Christian European colonizers.

Maybe this sounds a little confusing, because we associate many parts of the world—especially the Global South—with Christianity, including forms of Christianity that developed outside and beyond Western Europe. The African continent gave birth to many forms of indigenous and ancient Christianities, including Coptic Christianity in Egypt, which is nearly as old as Christianity itself. Catholicism runs rampant all over Central and South America. So why do we imagine "the West" as Europe, the United States, and Canada, to the exclusion of Native people in the US and everybody in the entirety of Mexico and Central and South America?

We'll talk more about this in the next chapter, but the answer here (and to many, many questions that boil down to "Wait, why is this so messed up?") is race. Christianity's imperial mission is also one of establishing and enforcing white supremacy. The presence of indigenous Christianities on the continent of Africa did not prevent white European Christian empires from colonizing, exploiting, and enslaving fellow Christians. Nor did the presence and persistence of Muslims throughout Europe mean that white European Christian empires consider those European Muslims part of the West. Muslims, even the ones living in Europe, can never be fully part of the West, because white European Christian imperial logic renders them part of the Muslim world.

Islam and the idea of a "Muslim world" help us see how the world religions paradigm is not about neutral definitions of what (or who) makes a religion, but rather about promoting (and enforcing!) the assumed inherent superiority of white European Christians and their

RELIGION IS GLOBAL ▪ **53**

empires. The world religions paradigm holds all other groups we now call "religions" up to the yardstick of white European Christianity and finds them wanting. And the world religions paradigm just *loves* to use Islam as an example of a religion that just doesn't quite measure up.

Islam is and has always been a global religion, right from its start. Within a century of Muhammad's life (570–632 CE), Muslim communities emerged across north Africa, throughout the Middle East and the Arabian Peninsula, and into Southwest Asia. Communities practiced Islam as far east as India and China as early as the beginning of the eighth century CE; as far south and east as Southern and Eastern Africa in the ninth and tenth centuries CE; and as far west as the Iberian Peninsula starting in the early eighth century CE. Islam developed across Africa, Asia, and Southern Europe in the centuries that followed largely due to Muslim traders' nautical superiority in the Indian Ocean and Mediterranean. (It was European Christians, after all, who thought the earth was flat and compasses weren't real.) Transatlantic slavers forced Black Africans to the so-called New World; scholars estimate that some 10 to 20 percent of these were Muslims. Which means the presence of Black Muslims on this continent pre-dates the existence of a United States. (More on that in the next chapter, too.)

Muslims have lived all over the world for nearly as long as Islam has existed. So for the world religions paradigm to exclude Islam from "Western religions," "Western religions" has to be about something other than geography. And it is. You know by now that "Western religions" means "religion done by white Christians." In the world religions model, Muslims are literally from a whole new world, one fundamentally and irrevocably other than and incompatible with—indeed, hostile to—Western civilization.

Thus, Islam being not-Western has nothing to do with where Muslims live, where Islam started, or where it is practiced. Morocco, a Muslim majority country, is farther west than Spain, a predominantly Christian country. More Muslims live in Asia than anywhere else in the world, but most Americans think of Islam as a Middle Eastern religion rather than an Eastern one. Speaking of which: What is the Middle East in the middle of? Because we live on a ball. The surface of a ball has no middle. What the heck does "Middle East" even mean?

It means that we've found the world religions paradigm at work again, friends. American and European military and financial interests have been drawing and redrawing the boundaries of the Middle East for centuries. But their decisions grew out of anxieties about Jerusalem being an "Eastern" city (when Judaism and Christianity—two traditions with close ties to Jerusalem—were so clearly *Western* religions) and about the brownness of Palestine (so white Christians needn't picture their savior in the image of the colonized).

The Middle East is only the middle of anything if you're measuring from Europe, which has designated itself "the West." This same small slice of the big round ball we live on gave birth to two Western religions, Christianity and Judaism, and one Eastern religion, Islam. The same spot on the globe can only be east and west at the same time if "east" and "west" are ideological distinctions and not geographical ones. Islam helps us see that the world religions paradigm divides religious traditions into major and minor based not on math (number of adherents, historical persistence, geographical coordinates) but on, well, vibes—the vibes in question being "How much does this community resemble white European Christianity?" and "Do they have stuff worth stealing?" Islam and concepts like the Muslim world show us that "world religions" and our sense of where specific religions live have a lot more to do with politics than they do with objective data analysis.

Which makes sense, to be honest. Because there's no such thing as raw data when it comes to people—guys with pens (and this includes us!) make choices about which parts of their findings to research and how to best convey what that research means, why it matters. And one of the clearest places to see the meaning made of Islam, Christianity, and world religions is on maps.

BORDERS ARE LIES WE TELL ON MAPS AND DEFEND WITH BOMBS

Because here's the thing, readers: maps are political. *All* maps are polit-ical. #YesAllMaps. How we choose to represent data is political—that is to say, it has stakes, it makes an argument. Maps represent choices made by interpreters of data. That data was collected and transmitted by folks who had their own reasons for collecting it, folks who wanted us to see the world in a very particular way.

Again, we live on a ball. Borders don't just happen; people make decisions about which land belongs to whom and why. As Ilyse likes to say, borders are lies we tell on maps and defend with bombs. People kill and die to control and cross those lies we tell on maps. And our sense of who belongs where, who can or cannot safely cross a lie told on a map, has a lot to do with—yep—religion.

One of the clearest examples of how maps reflect imperial force bolstered by the idea of religion is South Asia during and after British rule of the region—because the British Empire *literally redrew the region* according to its understanding of religious differences. That's right: we can directly trace the borders that exist in present-day South Asia to British imperial understandings of the world religions paradigm.

How is this even possible? Guns and pens once again, friends. Guns and pens.

The British Empire, for whom the sun never set, exerted direct and significant colonial and imperial control over South Asia from the mid-eighteenth century till the mid-twentieth century. (The Brits were there earlier and hung around after, but we're sticking to the height of their imperial control for this example.) British imperial maps of South Asia help us see the world religions paradigm—and the direct connection between imperialism and the idea of religion—in living color. (Or, just below, in black and white, because that's how publishing books works.) The guys with guns and the guys with pens were incredibly active, destructive, and productive in South Asia—and, ultimately, their ideas about religion literally redrew the world.

We're including a few early twentieth-century British imperial maps to show you what we mean.

These three maps—based directly on "Prevailing Religions," "Prevailing Religions: Hindus," and "Prevailing Religions: Muslims," but redrawn here for clarity—all cite the same data and were published in the 1909 *Imperial Gazetteer*. A gazetteer is a type of official index that records every piece of information that imperial officials collected and what that information meant. Gazetteers represent a significant genre of colonial and imperial publication; they were readily available, circulated the world over, and often reprinted in other books and media. Gazetteers also literally prove Edward Said's point: when colonizers showed up, they brought guys with guns (armies) and guys with pens (the scholars writing these gazetteers with the express intent to circulate knowledge about the colonies at home to government officials, policy makers, the ruling classes, and the educated elite). In the case of these maps, the guys with pens collected data on South Asian colonial subjects and represented their findings cartographically.

Do us a favor and take a minute to look at these maps with us— really look at them. What stands out to you? What do these maps tell us about religion? About Hinduism? About Islam? Are you surprised by what you're seeing? Why or why not?

We told you that maps are political—that maps don't just convey data; they interpret and make meaning of it for readers. So let's think about what meanings these maps are making of religion.

When we look at map 1, we see decisions that mapmakers made about what religion is, which religions matter, and where religion and religions fit in the world. Each region is shown as belonging to one and only one religion, despite many people in South Asia practicing rituals and holding commitments to multiple traditions and people of all religious traditions living in all parts of South Asia. "Prevailing Religions" divides regions of South Asia along religious lines; the color of each region, in the original, and the shadings in this version denote

MAP I

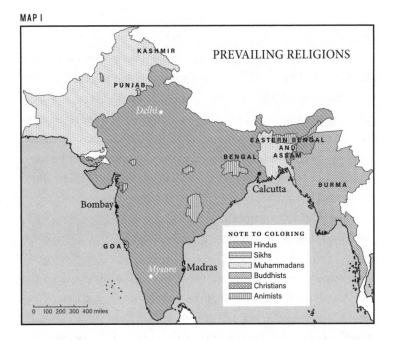

a different religion.* The map depicts "Muhammadans" (an archaic and problematic term for Muslims), Hindus, Christians, Sikhs, Buddhists, and animists (another archaic and racialized term that, in the world religions model, is often reserved for Native religious practices of varying origin). As you explore the map, the most important thing to note is this: one region = one color/pattern = one religion. This map makes religious belonging singular, bounded, and simple (when, as you know from the introduction of this book, religion is messy because people are messy). This map tells readers that huge tracts of land have one uniform religion.

---

*The original maps were widely distributed in the early twentieth century and beyond but are now public domain images. We had the maps redrawn for print clarity in this very book, but you can find the original images on our website: keepingit101.com/rindwy.

"Prevailing Religions" tells us that most of South Asia is Hindu (diagonal stripes); wee corners of the subcontinent are Muslim (gray dots); Christianity (crosshatched pattern) is stashed in Goa, a city that never had a majority Christian population but was controlled by the Portuguese for a hot minute. So-called animists (vertical stripes) reflect regions populated by uncasted majorities whom British scholars could never quite make sense of or, in some cases, gain unfettered access to. Buddhism (checkerboard pattern) forms a border between what British imperial records call "India" and "Burma." Sikhs are in the legend, but you *really* have to work to find that small section on this map (horizontal stripes).

Take a minute, we'll wait.

Did you find it?

There's a teeny tiny section where the diagonal stripes meets the grey dots in the top left corner of the map. It's in a region called Punjab—a region, by the way, far more expansive than the horizontally striped section itself—that had been majority Sikh for nearly half a millennium by the time the *Imperial Gazetteer* published "Prevailing Religions." Remember when we said Sikhi falls out of the world religions model? It's also practically falling right off this map.

We'll come back to Sikhi and Punjab in the next section. For now, look at maps 2 and 3.

These maps use the same data as the "Prevailing Religions" map, but, as you can see, the cartographers are making different meanings of that data. "Prevailing Religions" makes it seem as though each region has only one religion. "Prevailing Religions: Hindus" and "Prevailing Religions: Muslims" tell a different story, one that—correctly—shows Hindus and Muslims living in the same regions all over the subcontinent. If you look closely, you'll see that some of the regions the original "Prevailing Religions" map coded as Hindu were, in fact, 50-plus percent Muslim. "Prevailing Religions: Hindus" also uses gradations in much broader strokes than does "Prevailing Religions: Muslims,"

MAP 2

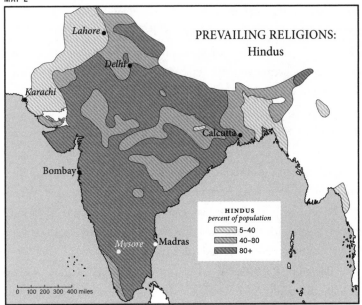

Lahore

Delhi

Karachi

PREVAILING RELIGIONS:
Hindus

Calcutta

Bombay

HINDUS
percent of population
5–40
40–80
80+

Mysore Madras

0 100 200 300 400 miles

MAP 3

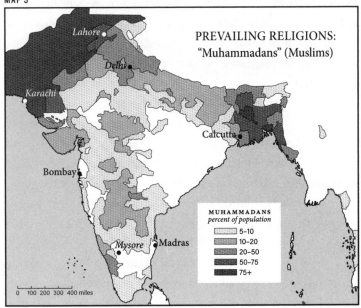

Lahore

Delhi

Karachi

PREVAILING RELIGIONS:
"Muhammadans" (Muslims)

Calcutta

Bombay

MUHAMMADANS
percent of population
5–10
10–20
20–50
50–75
75+

Mysore Madras

0 100 200 300 400 miles

deemphasizing the size and scope of South Asian Muslim populations while highlighting if not exaggerating Hindu dominance. "Prevailing Religions: Muslims" also strongly implies that most Muslims in the region were concentrated at the top corners of the subcontinent—places we now know as Pakistan and Bangladesh.

As we've been saying: maps are arguments. Maps are political. These maps are British imperial arguments for South Asia as inherently, inarguably Hindu—despite the widespread prevalence of Muslims throughout the entire region. These maps argue that one region = one religion, even as they demonstrate more nuance than that. When the British, authors of this map, came to partition South Asia into nation-states with the idea that one nation = one religion, these very maps—among others—helped mark those borders.

"Prevailing Religions" is also an argument for significant Christian influence in South Asia. We noted that Goa is marked predominantly Christian, despite that region never having a majority Christian population. That demarcation is a political choice, a claim that Christianity had established a stronghold in India. That claim is false. There have been Christians in India for a very long time, but Christianity has never been the *dominant* religion in any major sector of South Asia. The claim this map makes is supported, not by data, but by a worldview that values Christianity above all other religions.

All three "Prevailing" maps draw on the same kind of Eurocentric Christian imperialist white supremacist logic that created the world religions paradigm. Empires don't make maps because they're hungry for knowledge; empires make maps to divide and conquer the globe. These maps show us in no uncertain terms that the British empire used religion to redraw the world.

EMPIRE? STRIKE BACK!

So, as you can see, maps and mapping aren't neutral intellectual exercises. Maps teach us what meaning we should make of the data they represent and—whether it's immediately clear to us or not—how we should act on that data. Mapping is a subtle but significant exercise of imperial force.

British imperial forces used the world religions paradigm to create new borders, new *countries*, in South Asia—and the borders they created, depicted on the maps we just showed you and so many others like them, absolutely furthered British colonial interests. Cartographers created these maps to convince readers that Hindus and Muslims were not one population occupying the same region together for centuries, but rather two irreconcilably different peoples—different *religions*—that must have their own separate regions to keep the peace. We've said that maps are arguments, but maps like these aren't just for British imperial officials. They were never marked "For Internal Use Only." They were circulated, studied, presented as incontrovertible fact everywhere the British could. Vitally, maps like these are meant to convince South Asian Hindus and Muslims that they are safer, better off, if they abide by the religious/political borders drawn for them by the Brits.

This is why Said argued the guys with pens were ultimately more dangerous than the guys with guns. Guys with guns? Sure, they can kill you. But guys with pens will teach you and your children that everything about you is wrong, lesser, *deserving* of domination, violence, even death. That the harms you experience under imperial domination are necessary, inevitable, and for your own good, actually. And they *can* do this precisely because under imperialism, both after and while the guys with guns demonstrate that they *will* kill you, the guys with pens control everything: schools, laws, policies, rights and your access to them, access to movement, whole economies. This is a system that wants to be—strives to be—totalizing.

This kind of imperial force is what revolutionary philosopher Frantz Fanon called "the colonization of the mind." Imperial force presents its stereotypes, its language, its policies, its practices as superior—markers of civilization, of humanity. Colonized peoples internalize these ways of thinking and being, learning that they are inferior, less civilized, less human. Empires instill their attitudes, practices, aesthetics, and values through systems like laws, schools, businesses, and popular culture.

The British invaded India only to declare Muslims violent invaders of a region that should (they said) be properly understood as Hindu. Imperial officials insisted that religion—which they imagined as singular and discreet, rather than the big old mess we know it to be—was the best lens through which to understand South Asia. And when World War II exhausted British resources so far as to necessitate the dissolution of its empire, they used religion to divide the subcontinent (among other places) along religious lines.

Watch the world religions paradigm work.

You already know from our "Prevailing Religions" maps that Muslims lived all over the subcontinent in the beginning of the twentieth century. But in 1947, retreating colonizers redrew—or partitioned—the region in such a way to confine Muslim belonging to what would become East and West Pakistan, later Pakistan and Bangladesh. Dividing Pakistani Muslims from Indian Hindus, they argued, was necessary for peace.

Here's the thing about telling people they can't stay in places their families have lived for centuries, though: it never unfolds peacefully. It wasn't only Hindus and Muslims harmed by the world religions model in action, either; Buddhists were largely relegated to Sri Lanka, Burma (Myanmar), and mostly independent Nepal. And what about Sikhs, you might be wondering? We told you that Punjab had been a majority Sikh region for centuries, but Partition did not formally designate Punjab a Sikh state. In the same way that Sikhi drops out of the world religions model, Sikhs fall off the map of South Asia after Indian independence. Partition affected South Asians from *all* religious backgrounds, many of whom died or were forcibly relocated as a result of this imperial remapping project.

The violence of religion, empire, and maps continues in South Asia to this day—and we can see that violence perhaps most clearly in the regions of Jammu and Kashmir, whose boundaries are still hotly contested by India and Pakistan. Remember when we told you that the world religions paradigm is inconsistent, that it doesn't even abide by its own rules? Jammu and Kashmir are excellent examples of this. Both Jammu and Kashmir were and are Muslim-majority regions. So, if we follow the logic of British imperialism—religion = borders = nations—that territory would belong to Muslim-majority Pakistan, right?

Pakistan certainly thought so, but the nascent, majority-Hindu state of India vehemently disagreed, citing and wielding historic British support for Hindu administration of the region. To this day, Jammu and Kashmir are still claimed *and formally administered* by both India *and* Pakistan; Kashmiris are neither fully Indian nor fully Pakistani, and Kashmir's religious identities are viewed as problematic to each state. (Of course Muslims and Hindus live in both India and Pakistan, which is why we keep telling you the world religions paradigm is sus.)

This is also why Jammu and Kashmir were and are quite literally unmappable. Google Maps will not define the borders of the region because both India and Pakistan continue to lay claim to the territory. Google does not want to cause an international incident by accepting either side's borders. So, when we say Jammu and Kashmir are unmappable, we mean they literally do not appear on the most widely used mapping tool in the entire world. And, as more than half of the world's population uses Google, half of the *entire world* is using a platform that's still being shaped by the world religions paradigm, still being defined and literally drawn by Western European imperial definitions of religion.

■ ■ ■

We've focused on South Asia in this chapter, but these imperial shenanigans are still happening the world over. The world religions paradigm physically shaped South Asia, but its effects are much more global than that. Religious differences, interpreted through this Western European imperial way of defining, dividing, and conquering the world also helped draw boundaries in what is now Palestine/Israel, informed the emergence of post-Soviet nations in Eastern Europe and Central Asia, even helped create states in what became the US. In all of these places, the world religions paradigm helped further imperial agendas, driven by assumptions that one land = one people = one religion, even though everything everywhere has always been more complicated than maps make it out to look.

But religion is never *only* imperial. Peoples all over the world use religion to survive, disrupt, and resist empire (with mixed results) in the wake of colonialism and imperialism. The world religions model helps us understand that religion is a technology of empire, enforcing white European Christian imperial attitudes all over the world, historically and today. And as we'll see in the next chapter, these global flows of power and culture shaped and continue to shape standards, attitudes, assumptions, and policies about human bodies, what they mean, and how we should use them.

■ ■ ■ ■ ■ ■ ■ ■ ■ ■

FURTHER READING

Talal Asad, *Genealogies of Religion: Discipline and Reasons of Power in Christianity and Islam* (Baltimore, MD: Johns Hopkins University Press, 1997)

Cemil Aydin, *The Idea of the Muslim World: A Global Intellectual History* (Cambridge, MA: Harvard University Press, 2019)

Frantz Fanon, *Black Skin, White Masks* (New York: Grove, 1967)

Peter Gottschalk, *Religion, Science, and Empire: Classifying Hinduism and Islam in British India* (New York: Oxford University Press, 2012)

Tomoko Masuzawa, *The Invention of World Religions; or, How European Universalism Was Preserved in the Language of Pluralism* (Chicago: University of Chicago Press, 2007)

Ilyse R. Morgenstein Fuerst, *Indian Muslim Minorities and the 1857 Rebellion: Religion, Rebels, and Jihad* (London: Bloomsbury Academic, 2020)

Junaid Rana, "The Story of Islamophobia," *Souls* 9, no. 2 (2007)

Edward W. Said, *Orientalism* (New York: Vintage, 1978)

Jonathan Z. Smith, "Religion, Religions, Religious," in *Relating Religion: Essays in the Study of Religion* (Chicago: University of Chicago Press, 2004)

FURTHER LISTENING ON KEEPING IT 101

(E102) "Who Gets Left Out of 'Religion'?"

(E401) "World Religions, but Better"

(E409) "You Still Don't Know About Islam, Part 1"

CHAPTER 3

RACE IS (MADE OF) RELIGION

*in which we show you why if you're
not thinking about race,
you're not understanding religion*

In the last chapter, we told you religion is a tool of Western European empire, that religion works in concert with other modern constructs like science to justify and perpetuate Western European imperial expansion and dominion, and that empires use religion to draw borders and make nations. But those operations of religion aren't unique to Western Europe, even though they have deep roots there. We are talking, of course, about what's now the United States of America—and how it became a nation by using religion (specifically white Western European Christianity) to literally create race in an American context.

You read that correctly: America built *race* out of *religion* in order to secure its economic independence from another empire (the British one). Western European Christians in the "new world" (new to whom—Columbus?) used religion and science to explain why they were spiritually and biologically superior to, and thus could own and murder, people they determined to be not-white. These same Christians of Western European descent, newly self-proclaimed-white, used the economic spoils of this exploitation and butchery to create what is now the United States of America. Religion: once again redrawing maps to protect and further white Western imperial interests.

That's a lot of big ideas in a few short paragraphs. Let's start with the basics.

▪ ▪ ▪

Depending on the circumstances that led you to this book, the title of this chapter is probably either a "Duh" or a "What in the what???" moment. For folks who have to pay attention to race in order to stay alive—that is, for anyone *not* taught to think they are white—"You have to think about race to understand religion" is so obvious that it might seem incredible we need to say it at all. So let us use our "I" statements: Megan did two master's degrees and a whole PhD without being required to think critically about race. She read some books and took some classes with folks who *do* think critically about race, of course! But at the top of this chapter, we need you to know that it is fully possible and, indeed, statistically common, to earn a doctorate in American religions without proving you know one (1) thing about race and its relationship to American religion.

Folks for whom "you need to think about race to understand religion" is old news, we completely understand the impulse to skip to the next chapter. (Please don't, though.) Folks for whom this is brand new information, let's set some ground rules.

It is okay—not great! not ideal! but okay—that you didn't know this before. You know now, and you'll know even more if you keep reading. Before you do, we'd love for you to pause a moment and be curious about *why* you didn't need to know. Who benefits from white folks not paying attention to race? Other white folks and systems that privilege whiteness, right? That's not justice, and that's not the world we want to build. So let's think about how to move forward from here.

Maybe you feel frustrated or guilty or even angry that you missed how important race is and how much damage it does. Those feelings are a) valid and b) not interesting to folks for whom paying attention to race is a necessary strategy if they want to continue breathing. Feel your feels; share them with other folks who learned to think they are white (and *only* those folks!); and direct that frustration or guilt or anger in directions where your whiteness can help more people get more justice.

That's the goal of this chapter and also this book. We want you to

- understand that people make race (not the other way around)
- see that religion is a big part of how people, and especially Americans, made and continue to make race
- learn about how Native peoples' relationship to race and religion teaches us something important about the work religion does in what's now the United States

Obviously American religion is shaped by more than just race. (We'll talk more about intersectionality in a moment, and more about sexuality in the next chapter.) For now, we're primarily focusing on race because we want you to trace how European Christian imperialism spread across the Atlantic Ocean and the United States became an empire in its own right—in large part by making race out of religion.

Learning more about religion and how it makes race isn't virtue signaling: it's scholarship. Your understanding of religion is not just incomplete if you don't think about race; it is fundamentally broken. Religion and race work in related ways—but also with some significant differences—all over the world. But we can't fit the whole world in this chapter and we all have to start somewhere. So: learning how religion helped make race in America can be a first step toward repairing not just your own knowledge, but your complicity in systems that privilege whiteness and your relationship with the rest of the world.

MAKING RACE

We talked a little bit about social constructs in the first chapter, but in case you've skipped ahead . . .

Religion is a social construct: a system that sorts humans into categories to maintain existing social hierarchies. Humans with power make systems to preserve, protect, and expand that power. Which means the categories humans sort each other into aren't just groups; they're rankings. The more you're like the people with the most power? The more likely you are to be able to access the safety, resources, and advantages of that powerful group. Religion, race, gender, sexuality, class, and ability are some of the major socially constructed groups that humans sort ourselves into.

There is no getting outside of or discarding these socially constructed categories. This isn't to say that identities assigned at birth are the best descriptors of who we are as individuals, despite the public vitriol of wizardly inclined billionaires. Individual people express their individual identities in ways that bend and break socially constructed categories all the time! (*Keeping It 101* has an entire episode on *RuPaul's Drag Race*, if you want to hear us nerd out about what gender theorist Judith Butler calls "insubordination.") But bending or breaking categories still keeps you in relationship with those categories.

We've been saying all along that religion is what people do. And we just told you that no one exists outside socially constructed categories of identity. Which means that

a. all people have race
b. all people doing religion have race

More specifically, existing systems and institutions—created by those guys with pens from chapter 2—*assign* people to a racialized category of belonging. We'll come back to this in the next section. For now, let's start by saying you have to think about race to understand religion, because everyone doing religion has race.

But it's more complicated than that. No social construct exists in a vacuum, because people are never just one thing. Our selves are made up of a jumble of identities that influence our proximity to or distance from certain kinds of privilege—that is, unearned and often unconscious material and social advantages experienced at the expense of others' systemic disadvantage.

The "unconscious" part is where a lot of folks get tripped up, but you don't have to *know* you're benefiting from someone else's oppression to reap the rewards of an unjust system. What's more, you don't have to know you're perpetuating an unjust system in order to help injustice flourish. Employers, for example, might talk about "fit" or "office culture" without even realizing their tendency toward hiring folks who look (act, speak, dress, etc.) just like them. This isn't to excuse racist, sexist, classist, queerphobic, or ableist hiring practices or oppressive practices of any kind. Rather, we hope this inspires you to get curious about how, where, and—most importantly—*why* you feel more or less comfortable, more or less at ease in different kinds of company. For extra credit, give some thought to what kind of systems get built for the comfort and ease of those controlling the systems, and at what cost to other humans.

When systems and institutions privilege one group of people to the material and social disadvantage of other groups of people, this is oppression. Oppression is not about individuals, which is why Ilyse and Megan tend to make grumpy noises when someone says something like "But I don't *feel* oppressed." Oppression isn't about feelings. Oppression is about math. Which group benefits the most from existing systems and thus fights hardest to preserve those systems? Which groups cannot consistently access material and social benefits as a result of the dominant group's privilege? Think about how many transgender presidents the US has elected, or how many

Black women CEOs head up Fortune 500 companies. Oppression is injustice you can count.

It's possible to experience privilege through certain aspects of one's identity while experiencing oppression because of other parts of your identity. As Megan explains to her students: she's not white on Monday, a lady on Tuesday, queer on Wednesday, disabled on Thursday, and witchy on Friday. Her weeks don't start with White Privilege Mondays followed by four days of oppression and a break from being perceived on the weekends. All of those pieces of her identity always are happening all at once. This overlapping messy matrix of privilege and oppression is what attorney and preeminent critical race theorist Kimberlé Crenshaw termed "intersectionality."

Identities that confer privilege and oppression are social constructs. People created them to explain why small groups of humans deserve easier, better, safer lives than all other groups of humans. But the fact that these modes of belonging are socially constructed does not mean they are fake or unimportant. Vectors of privilege and oppression like race have very real and emphatically material consequences. As cultural critic Ta-Nehisi Coates wrote to his son,

> All our phrasing—race relations, racial chasm, racial justice, racial profiling, white privilege, even white supremacy—serves to obscure that racism is a visceral experience, that it dislodges brains, blocks airways, rips muscle, extracts organs, cracks bones, breaks teeth. You must never look away from this. You must always remember that the sociology, the history, the economics, the graphs, the charts, the regressions all land, with great violence, upon the body. (2015)

Social constructs are ways we make sense of our bodies and the bodies of others—but those socially constructed hierarchies land, as Coates says, "with great violence upon the body." The stakes of socially constructed identities run frighteningly high. People murder other people for doing race "wrong," as Black Oklahomans experienced in the Tulsa Race Massacre of 1921. Governments steal land and give it to colonizers, as Japanese Americans experienced during World War II and Native peoples in the United States and all over the world are still experiencing.

Because the stakes of identity are so high, it can be hard to grapple with the fact that our identities are socially constructed, that we learn who we are and how we fit in the world from everyone and everything else around us. Identities like race and gender and sexuality *feel* natural, essential, and unchangeable. But anatomy is not destiny, no matter what Sigmund Freud said. Understandings of what bodies mean, what bodies are for, what bodies can and should be, change over time and space, just as the people who make meanings of their bodies and the bodies of others change over time and space.

When we talk about race in this book—just like when we talk about religion—we are talking about a *modern* social construct, a way of understanding the world and our place in it that emerges out of European Christian imperialism. As we discussed in chapter 2, European Christian imperialism has been shaping the entire globe (and its maps, as you might remember!) for roughly half a millennium. You probably already know that European Christian empires have some very specific ideas about whose bodies are best and what all bodies are for. European Christian empires put the missionary in "missionary position," after all!

It's important to remember that race, like religion, is a relatively new way of sorting humans into unequal groups. Like religion, our *contemporary* thinking about race dates back to about the seventeenth century. Which isn't to say that our understanding of race has been static over the past four hundred years! But thinking that skin tones, behaviors, languages and ways of speaking, foodways, attitudes, geographies, and demeanors can be distilled into a single, essential, unchanging identity that dictates who groups of people are and how much their country should value them? That concept of race has remained fairly consistent since the 1600s, even as popular understandings of which sort of people fit in which sort of racial category are in constant fluctuation. Whiteness in particular, as sociologist Tressie McMillam Cottom teaches us, is elastic: it expands and contracts to maintain its position at the top of America's racial hierarchy.

Whatever it says in the Declaration of Independence or the Constitution, America has from its inception conducted itself as a white Christian nation. White Christian nationalism doesn't just refer to explicitly white supremacist Christian groups like the Proud Boys or the Ku Klux Klan. Rather, white Christian nationalism acknowledges that America's systems and institutions privilege—were *built* to privilege—white Christian people and qualities we associate with white Christianity at every conceivable level. This, like all oppression, is about math. How many nonwhite non-Christian presidents have Americans elected? (None. The answer is zero.) How much does Walmart, a white Christian-owned company valued at over $400 billion, make every year—and how much do their exploitative labor practices cost the American people? (We'll save you the search: $6.2 billion in public assistance as of 2014.) When the Supreme Court defines religious freedom, who is most often protected? (More on that in the next chapter.) Host of NPR's *Code Switch* Gene Demby said that white supremacy is in America's source code—we're going to push that a step further. Religion, European imperialism's weapon of choice, *created* American whiteness and *wrote* white Christian nationalism as America's source code.

But the story of race, religion, and the United States is about so much more than just whiteness, Christianity, and oppression. While based in exploitative economies, race also creates community, culture, joy, radical resistance, and new ways of understanding and being in the world. The complexity and ambivalence of race—race's foundation in European Christian imperialism, the liberatory spaces and acts it makes possible—are precisely why you need to think about race to understand religion, in the United States and elsewhere.

RACE = RELIGION + CAPITALISM + SCIENCE

You already know that religion was and remains a powerful tool in the arsenal of imperialism. But what does religion have to do with race?

We explained in the last chapter that the concept of religion is—as theorist of race and religion Junaid Rana argues—inherently hostile toward Jews and Muslims, an imperial tool for the dehumanization and commodification of nonwhite non-European non-Christians. But this doesn't mean that religion does exactly the same work in all places or at all times after the concept's invention in the seventeenth century. As novelist L. P. Hartley puts it in *The Go-Between* (1953), we need to treat the past like a foreign country. They do things differently there and then.

So, when texts like the Hebrew Bible talk about people with darker skin, we cannot assume that the writers of that text or the characters in the story mean what Americans mean when they call themselves (or are called) Black or Native or Asian or Latinx. What race and religion mean and what those categories do varies according to geography and history. In the United States, Rana argues, religion as a category should also be understood as not only anti-Muslim and anti-Jewish, but also as anti-Black and anti-Native. Scholar of race and American religion Kathryn Gin Lum would add that US religion is also anti-Asian. To put it more plainly: as it functions and has always functioned in the United States, religion supports the supremacy of white Christians over all other peoples. Or, if you're into that whole brevity thing, American religion is a tool of white Christian nationalism.

Let's get this clear from the start: this does *not* mean that Black, Native, Asian, and other nonwhite Americans can't or don't do religion. Of course they do! But when it comes to how religion works systemically—that is, within and through systems—America as a nation-state tends to use religion to protect its own imperial agenda. Yes, some minoritized communities have successfully appealed for religious protections. But when we're talking about the United States, "religion" without a modifier assumes white Christianity. America's protections for religion mostly tend to protect the folks with the most preexisting privilege (white mainstream Christians) to codify and bolster the idea that "real" Americans are white and Christian (white Christian nationalism).

Sexuality further complicates systemic religious protections; we'll talk more in the next chapter about how religion shapes the systems (like healthcare and the courts) that police and control our bodies. First we want to walk you through how race and religion became so entangled in the United States. And boy, are race and religion ever tangled up in red, white, and blue! But more than that: race and religion are co-constitutive in America. Race and religion make and remake each other. Which is why, as the title of this chapter says, if you're not thinking about race? You're not understanding religion.

We need to start our consideration of race, religion, and the United States by highlighting two practices implemented by European Christian empires: settler colonialism and chattel slavery. These practices, made possible by the Doctrine of Discovery, are the twin pillars of American imperialism. Chattel slavery and settler colonialism set American understandings of race apart from how categories like Blackness or Nativeness function in other parts of the world. So, before we slalom through the religious origins of race in the United States, let's make sure we're all on the same page about these key terms.

As you might remember from chapter 2, the Doctrine of Discovery exhorts European Christian empires to go forth and conquer the whole world for Christ. The Doctrine of Discovery declared all land not inhabited by Christians to be terra nullius, unoccupied land—which is Latin for "The Roman Catholic Church voided the humanity of all non-Christians." From the fifteenth through the nineteenth century, the Spanish and Portuguese empires conquered the "New World" under the imprimatur of the Roman Catholic Church.

The Spanish used religion in what's now the United States like they did everywhere else: as a shield and a cudgel to expand their emphatically Roman Catholic empire. Upon arrival in the so-called New World, conquistadors and missionaries would read the *Requerimiento*, a declaration (in Latin, which Native peoples generally did not speak) that the Roman Catholic pope was the rightful sovereign of the entire world. Yes, really. We told you all this noise was about empire. Native folks could either submit to imperial subjugation or face murder, enslavement, or torture. (Spoilers: the Spanish empire murdered, enslaved, and tortured Native people who submitted, too.) From Native peoples' first contact with European imperial force, "religion" meant domination, violence, and erasure.

By the sixteenth century, the British and French empires were also claiming colonized and precontact territory in what's now North America. Though Britain no longer owed allegiance to the pope, nevertheless she persisted in the proud Catholic tradition of seizing unempired lands and humans for Christ. As in South Asia, imperial expansion across the Atlantic deployed guys with guns and guys with pens. After benefiting from Native science—such as knowledge about how to find food and not freeze to death in the winter, for starters—to survive their initial colonizing wave, the guys with guns worked to eradicate as many of the people already living in the so-called New World as they could so that invading European Christians could claim as much post-genocidal territory as possible.

We talked about colonialism as a strategy of imperial force in the previous chapter, but it's important to understand what sets settler colonialism apart. All colonizers set up long-term settlements in the land they steal. All colonies keep government officials, militaries, and corporations behind to manage and profit off their stolen land, resources, and humans. But the colony isn't *home* for these businesses, soldiers, and government wonks. Settler colonialism takes this violence a step further, removing and often eradicating existing populations so that colonizers can establish themselves as the primary and rightful occupants of the territory. Settler colonialism makes imperial agents into *settlers*—folks who do not just exploit the colony but take it and make it their *home*.

In what's now the United States, the guys with guns first seized the land and murdered, terrorized, and forcibly converted the resident Native peoples. Then the guys with pens started teaching themselves and any remaining Native folks they *hadn't* murdered that forcible conversion is for Native people's own good, actually. All imperialism is about land theft, but settler colonialism combines land theft with culture theft (colonization of the mind, as Fanon called it) as a means to permanently replacing Indigenous peoples.

This "settler" distinction isn't just important for terminological accuracy—settler colonialism is a permanent substitution strategy. All colonialism requires mass murders, attempted genocides, official government policies and institutions designed to wipe Native peoples off the map. (Speaking of maps: Remember how we said mapping is a political act? Google just started showing Cherokee on its maps— which is to say nominally recognizing the sovereignty of the Cherokee Nation—in 2020.) But exploitation and violence are only steps along the way for settler colonialism. The goal of settler colonialism isn't domination: it's erasure and replacement.

The United States is an empire founded on European Christian settler colonialism. So, while many Americans assume that the Revolutionary War and the War of 1812 mark the *end* of colonization in North America, what we actually see is an exchange of one settler colonial regime for another. North Americans (US, Canadian, and Mexican) are still occupying Native lands. In fact, the US is still applying the Doctrine of Discovery when adjudicating Native land claims.

In addition to genocidal land theft, what became America built its economy on the transatlantic slave trade, centuries of European and later US empires enriching themselves through the capture, forcible transportation, and generational enslavement of African and Caribbean peoples. As with colonialism, slavery was not unique to the Americas—but the American version, chattel slavery, is particularly gruesome.

As advocates for American slavery argued, slavery is a biblical practice. Characters in the Hebrew and Christian Bibles were and owned slaves. (This doesn't mean we're suggesting that the owning of humans by other humans is ever okay because, and we cannot stress this enough, it is *not*.) In the Christian New Testament, Paul exhorts enslaved Christians to be subservient to their masters. In the Hebrew Bible, Noah curses the descendants of his son, Ham, with enslavement. But in other contexts, slavery was limited to the lifetime of the enslaved person; their children were not the property of slavers. In a chattel slavery system, slavers own not just the initially enslaved people but all of their descendants.

Chattel slavery directly shapes the way America came to understand race. The generational aspect of chattel slavery meant that any resemblance to enslaved people became proof of natural deficiencies. This is where science enters the chat. European and later American Christian imperialism claimed to have scientific proof of enslaved peoples' inherent, essential, unchangeable difference and inferiority. It was fine—beneficent, even!—for Christians to enslave non-Christians. After all, the pope himself had declared non-Christians subhuman through the doctrine of terra nullius. But you already know that religion as a tool of empire is rooted in hostility toward non-Christians.

Originally, European Christian colonizers—who would, decades later, declare themselves Americans—understood their distance, their superiority over enslaved African and Caribbean peoples and Native peoples, in fundamentally religious terms: the latter were "strangers" or "heathens." Either way the colonizers figured it, enslavement, eradication, and replacement by colonizers were for the best. But oppressed peoples are never only just victims of their own oppression—they have agency, the ability to act. Many Native folks converted to Christianity to survive, access resources, and help their communities. So, too, did enslaved people forcibly transported from Africa and the Caribbean.

Genocide and enslavement formed the backbone of America's emerging economy, so the newly fledged United States had little incentive to discontinue either practice. But how could they reconcile their empire's preferential option for Christianity with its economic dependence on genocide and slavery?

This is the beginning of America making race. As you know, race is a social construct, a way of ordering communities to create and maintain hierarchies—in this case, Euro-American Christian dominion over heathens and strangers, even after they'd converted to Christianity. In what was becoming the United States, white men who owned lands and humans made scientific arguments for the essential inferiority of non-Europeans or, later, people of non-European descent.

This is not to say that colonizers hatched an intentional plot to explain away behaviors and practices they knew were evil. Or it's not only that, because people have been criticizing the removal and replacement of Native people and arguing against the forcible transportation and enslavement of African and Caribbean people since either practice began. But these genocidal enslavers needed to solve the problem of sharing a religion with the people they had enslaved and tried to replace.

So colonizers drew on the tools they had at hand: religious, scientific, and imperial logics. Settler colonizers explained to themselves and their victims that even after conversion, there's something a little bit less sacred, a little bit (to a lot) less human about Christianity when it's done by non-Europeans. That explanatory framework of essential, incontrovertible, inheritable difference? That's race.

When we're talking about the creation of race out of religion, we don't only mean "This is when people started being treated poorly based on characteristics and traits assigned to them by imperial scientific racism," although that's obviously happening, too. But, equally as important, settler-colonizing European Christianity is how the folks we now think of as Americans learned to think they ("they" here includes your humble authors) were white. Race might *feel* natural, but it is absolutely made on and through bodies, including the bodies of people who—as James Baldwin writes—were taught to think they are white. Whiteness, Baldwin insists, is not a natural state of being but a *moral* choice, "for there are," he says, "no white *people*" ("On Being White and Other Lies," 1984).

This moment in American colonial history is when Christian settler-colonizers of European descent learned to think they were white, learned to think whiteness was superior to all other racial expressions, and used whiteness to justify more Christian imperialism and violence. We built America out of religion and race, and specifically through an economy of white Christian nationalism—that is, the conviction that America is and should be for white Christians. Even before it became "the United States," this country emerged out of principles of racialized religious superiority and "freedom," but not for everybody. As American religious historian Sylvester Johnson reminds us in *African American Religions* (2015), freedom for some requires the unfreedom of others. America's founders made a moral choice to believe they were white and used religion to construct, to *make*, race.

While race and religion are demonstrably rooted in American histories of exploitative and murderous Christian imperialism, we are not fully understanding religion and race if we focus solely on violence and oppression. The creation of American Blackness, for example, also makes space for creativity and escape and community and joy.

It should go without saying, but: Black Americans have used religion to reimagine themselves, their history, and the world outside legacies of violence and oppression. This does not, however, excuse or cancel out enslavement or white Christian nationalism. Nevertheless, like all oppressed peoples, people taught to think they were Black made a way out of no way and cultivated strategies of resistance and flourishing.

American history is full of Black resilience and creativity, if you know where and how to look for it. And religion has played a huge role in this work. We can see this in Nat Turner's prophecy-turned-rebellion and enslaved Black women's religion-making in domestic spaces (check out Alexis Wells-Oghoghomeh's *The Souls of Womenfolk* [2021] for more on this), to name only two of many examples.

But we'd like to tarry a moment with Sojourner Truth, an enslaved Black woman who emancipated herself and dedicated the rest of her life to freeing others. She is perhaps best known for her powerful speech supporting women's right to vote, which she delivered at the Woman's Rights Convention in Akron, Ohio, on May 29, 1851. You might know this speech as "Ain't I a Woman," though Truth certainly wouldn't.

Though illiterate, Truth was well educated, and not just for a formerly enslaved woman in mid-nineteenth-century America. Her first language was Dutch; her spoken English was formal, deliberate, evocative. So maybe you can imagine her posthumous surprise that the best known version of her speech has her sounding more like Butterfly McQueen in *Gone with the Wind* than Abraham Lincoln.

We've included a side-by-side comparison of the speech transcript *Anti-Slavery Bugle* journalist Marius Robinson published on June 21, 1851, and the version Frances Gage—an abolitionist, a white feminist, and a suffragist better known as "Aunt Fanny"—published in the *New York Independent* on April 23, 1863. (All the emphases are ours.)

The 1863 version—again, provided by white feminist abolitionist Aunt Fanny—uses the N-word. A lot. We have reproduced that slur here because it is vital that you see the racialized and racist ways that white Christian American women used Truth's work toward their own ends.

While you read the *Anti-Slavery Bugle* (left) and *New York Independent* (right) versions together (figure 1)*, note that *only* the latter version, provided by a white feminist abolitionist suffragist, uses that slur. What does this superficially nice, good white Christian woman's word choice—because it is clearly a choice—tell us about white Christian feminists' use of Truth's actual speech?

FIGURE 1: SOJOURNER TRUTH TRANSCRIPTS

Anti-Slavery Bugle (1851)	*New York Independent* (1863)
May I say a few words? I want to say a few words about this matter.	Well, chillen, whar dar's so much racket dar must be som'ting out o'kilter.
I am a woman's rights.	I tink dat, 'twixt de niggers of de South and de women at de Norf, all a-talking 'bout rights, de white men will be in a fix pretty soon.
(a) I have as much muscle as any man, and can do as much work as any man.	But what's all this here talking 'bout?
(b) I have plowed and reaped and husked and chopped and mowed, and can any man do more than that?	Dat man ober dar say dat women needs to be helped into carriages, and lifted over ditches, and to have de best place eberywhar.
I have heard much about the sexes being equal; I can carry as much as any man, and can (c) eat as much too, if (d) I can get it.	Nobody eber helps me into carriages or ober mud-puddles, or gives me any best place.
I am as strong as any man that is now.	And ar'n't I a woman?

* These texts and more are available through the Sojourner Truth Project: https://www.thesojournertruthproject.com/compare-the-speeches/.

Anti-Slavery Bugle (1851)	*New York Independent* (1863)
As for intellect, all I can say is, (e) if women have a pint and man a quart—why can't she have her little pint full?	Look at me.
You need not be afraid to give us our rights for fear we will take too much, for we can't take more than our pint'll hold.	(a) Look at my arm.
The poor men seem to be all in confusion, and don't know what to do.	(b) I have plowed and planted and gathered into barns, and no man could head me.
Why children, if you have woman's rights, give it to her and you will feel better.	and ar'n't I a woman?
You will have your own rights, and they wont be so much trouble.	I could work as much as (c) eat as much as a man, (when (d) I could get it,) and bear de lash as well
I can't read, but I can hear.	and ar'n't I a woman?
I have heard the bible and have learned that Eve caused man to sin.	I have borne thirteen chillen, and seen 'em mos' all sold off into slavery, and when I cried out with a mother's grief, none but Jesus heard
Well if woman upset the world, do give her a chance to set it right side up again.	and ar'n't I a woman?
The Lady has spoken about Jesus, how he never spurned woman from him, and she was right.	Den dey talks 'bout dis ting in de head.
When Lazarus died, Mary and Martha came to him with faith and love and besought him to raise their brother.	What dis dey call it?

continues

Anti-Slavery Bugle (1851)	*New York Independent* (1863)
And Jesus wept—and Lazarus came forth.	Dat's it, honey.
And how came Jesus into the world?	What's dat got to do with women's rights or niggers' rights?
(f) Through God who created him and woman who bore him.	(e) If my cup won't hold but a pint and yourn holds a quart, wouldn't ye be mean not to let me have a little half-measure full?
(g) Man, where is your part?	Den dat little man in black dar, he say women can't have as much rights as man 'cause Christ wa'n't a woman.
But the women are coming up blessed be God and a few of the men are coming up with them.	Whar did your Christ come from?
But man is in a tight place, the poor slave is on him, woman is coming on him, and he is surely between a hawk and a buzzard.	Whar did your Christ come from?
	(f) From God and a woman.
	(g) Man had nothing to do with him.
	If de fust woman God ever made was strong enough to turn de world upside down all her one lone, all dese togeder ought to be able to turn it back and git it right side up again, and now dey is asking to, de men better let 'em.
	Bleeged to ye for hearin' on me, and now ole Sojourner ha'n't got nothin' more to say.

In either version, Truth's oratorical prowess shines through. She is engaging in a thoroughly modern practice: exegesis, the interpretation and application of scripture in light of current events and conditions. This is a powerful and radical speech, in which Truth first claims the authority to interpret the Bible in front of a room full of white Christians and then claims common humanity with those white Christians. She declares all women—including herself, a self-emancipated Black woman—"blessed by God." This speech is brilliant, defiant, and uncompromising.

But for every audacious, radical claim made by a Black woman, there are a swarm of white ladies trying to profit off her labor while denying their common humanity. Which is precisely what we see in the condescending, down-homey patois in the *New York Independent*'s version of Truth. The Truth we get in the *Anti-Slavery Bugle* is poised, polished, erudite. The stereotypical patois that we see in the *New York Independent*—obviously offensive and troublingly racist—not only circulated much more broadly in its time but also is often, still, the only version Americans learn. We cannot overstate the magnitude of this hateful, settler colonialist revision. Truth did not talk like this. She talked like the *Anti-Racist Bugle* reports.

This racist rescripting of Truth's speech is one of the clearest examples we can give you of the legacies of settler colonialism. It is not just that Aunt Fanny misquotes Truth in the *New York Independent*. It's not even just that this racist version is the version most Americans would have heard or read in Truth's lifetime. "Ain't I a Woman" is, to this day, the version most Americans learn about (if they learn about Truth at all). Aunt Fanny and her descendants tried to *replace* the truth of Truth with a more convenient but less true truth that argues first and foremost for white women's rights. This is an argument rooted in white Christian nationalism, in convictions that freedom is the primary if not sole province of white Christian Americans.

We need you to see that this act of translation is just one of countless examples proving both that religion operates in service of empire (here, white American Christian nationalism) *and* that oppressed peoples are always finding ways to use religion in service of justice (as with Truth's bold exegetical assertion that she, a Black woman enslaved by white Christians, is a descendant of the mother of Christ—and that as such, she deserves public recognition of her full humanity). Without attending to the ambivalence and complexity of religion in this case study, we cannot fully appreciate the ways that, as James Baldwin wrote in his 1987 essay "To Crush the Serpent," "race and religion . . . are fearfully entangled in the guts of this nation, so profoundly that to speak of the one is to conjure up the other."

White Christian suffragists like Aunt Fanny or Harriet Beecher Stowe mobilized activists for their cause by using Truth's life and words. (Stowe called Truth "the Libyan Sibyl" in an interview published in the April 1863 issue of *The Atlantic*, and please be sure to note the racialized language in that headline. She might call Truth a prophet, but Stowe also *really* needs you to remember that Truth is Black.) But white Christian feminists, abolitionists, and suffragists mostly fell short of actual solidarity with their Black comrades—so much so that suffragists who vaunted Truth and others like her also insisted that white Christian women needed the vote to keep Black women in line.

Truth's Christianity was her own. Truth's God celebrated her Blackness, her womanness, and her faith in Jesus Christ. As you have seen, race and religion always function in the service of American empire. But that is not all race and religion have done or can do. The ambivalence of racialized religion—its creative potential for both oppression and liberation—becomes even clearer when we consider Native religions in what's now the United States.

RELIGION IS NOT A NATIVE CATEGORY

The name J. Z. Smith is probably starting to sound familiar by now; you might remember from chapter 1 his assertion that religion is not a native (small-n) category. Smith means that there is no such thing as an inherently religious person; religion has not always existed in all times in all places; "religion" is a Christian imperial way of categorizing human cultures, behaviors, and worldviews. But this means that religion is also not a capital-N Native category; religion was imposed upon Native peoples by colonizers. The organizing principles of many Native cultures do not fit neatly within the world religions paradigm.

As scholar of Native religions Abel Gomez put it in an October 2021 interview with *Interfaith America*, what we now think of as Native religions focus primarily on relationship, responsibility, and resurgence. Native peoples value, prioritize, and care for relationships with their family and ancestors, which includes their human communities (nations, tribes, and people), animal and spirit kindred, and the land itself. Because all of these—humans, animals, spirits, and lands—are their relations, Native people are responsible to and for them. And when we think about Native people, it's most important that we think of them in the present tense! That's what Gomez means by "resurgence."

The issue of Native resurgence is especially important because the world religions model assumed that the disappearance of Native peoples was both inevitable and desirable. After chapter 2, you know that the concept of religion and the world religions model are hierarchical: they sort and privilege groups of humans based on those groups' proximity and resemblance to Euro-American Christianity. But religion and the world religions model are also teleological, meaning they assume constant human progress and improvement. The Euro-American imperialist timeline for religion starts with animism or primitivism, what we would now think of as Native religions and African Traditional Religions, conceptualized as a loose but connected cluster of "unstructured" polytheisms. (If you know anything about Native or African Traditional Religions, you know that this timeline is already deeply wrong on just about every conceivable level. To give just one example: the Yoruban tradition Ifá is a highly sophisticated, beautifully intricate, and rigorously systematic way of being in the world that many now think of as religion. There could not be a more inaccurate way of describing Ifá than "unstructured.")

Religion, in the Euro-American imperial timeline, moves from animism and primitivism (yikes) toward "structured" polytheisms, like those of ancient Greece and Rome or contemporary Hinduism (double yikes), through "primitive" monotheisms like Judaism (just so very many yikeses). The timeline concludes with white Christianity as the natural and inevitable pinnacle of human civilization.

Do you see how this timeline makes race through religion and positions white Christians at the peak of human development? White Christian empires measure everyone else against themselves—selves they think of as inherently, scientifically superior to the rest of the world. These empires make a universalizing claim about religion: the world religions paradigm, the factually incorrect but effective assertion that religion has always been everywhere, and that *all* religions are second to *the* religion, Christianity. Then these empires use the systems they create to declare and govern all nonwhite non-Christians as fundamentally, essentially inferior. If one's religion is second, religious people are also second.

This is what we mean when we talk about the racialization of religion—the ways systems and institutions treat "doing religion" differently depending on who's doing the religion. Again, this model of religion and race isn't just a thought exercise. The racialization of religion—the making of race through religion, the remaking of religion through race—shapes, is still shaping, the United States. (Which is how the First Amendment of the US Constitution gets mobilized to protect white Christian evangelical anti-queer cake baking, for example, but not Native people using peyote in Native American Church ceremonies. More on both of these Supreme Court cases in a minute.) Racialized religion inspires and justifies policies intended to hasten what white Christian empires see as the inevitable, desirable, even necessary elimination of Native peoples. Eradicating and replacing Native peoples allowed white imperial Christianity to flourish in North America.

You already know that "religion" does the work of empire by affording more protection and privilege to those communities who most closely approximate the assumptions, aesthetics, and customs of white Christians. In the United States, we see religion work for empire through the American government's resolve to stamp out Native cultures, including Native religions. Until the 1978 American Indian Religious Freedom Act, the official policy of the United States was to, in the words of Army Captain Richard Henry Pratt, "kill the Indian in [Native people], and save the man." America's lawmakers, law interpreters, and law enforcers have always worked, are still working, against Native people's survival.

But, as you know, Native people have agency. Despite centuries of violent oppression, Native people were never docile or mindless subjects of Spanish, British, French, or US empires. Indigenous strategies of resistance emerged upon Native peoples' first contact with colonizers, as scholar of American empire Tisa Wenger argues in *We Have a Religion* (2009). Native resistance to empire continues to this day. The Ghost Dance Rebellion at Wounded Knee, the American Indian Movement's occupation of Alcatraz, and water protectors' opposition to the Dakota Access Pipeline are just a few important moments in Native people's refusal to surrender their commitments and their lives to America's white Christian nationalism.

In almost all of these instances, we see American institutions treat Native religion as something other and lesser than white Christianity. But we also see Native people using the category of religion to argue for their dignity, humanity, and survival. As with Black American religion, Native religion in what's now the US shows us the complicated and ambivalent function of religion in relationship to race.

Yankton Dakota writer and activist Zitkála Šá published a powerful piece addressing this complexity and ambivalence in the December 1902 issue of *The Atlantic.* In "Why I Am a Pagan," she writes,

> with a compassion for all echoes in human guise, I greet the solemn-faced "native preacher" whom I find awaiting me. I listen with respect for God's creature, though he mouth most strangely the jangling phrases of a bigoted creed. . . . I prefer to their [Christian] dogma my excursions into the natural gardens where the voice of the Great Spirit is heard in the twittering of birds, the rippling of mighty waters and the sweet breathing of flowers. If this is Paganism . . . I am a Pagan.

Zitkála Šá lays plain the function of American imperial Christianity: to convert her away from her sacred connection to her land and her people. But she does not reject the concept of religion; rather, she argues that she should be allowed to practice her own religion in her own way—an appeal to principles of religious freedom codified in America's founding documents.

Zitkála Šá's rhetoric is pacifying. One might even say civil. But the critique underlying her tone is searing. She survived America's residential school system, a state-sponsored religious campaign of terror that attempted to eradicate Native culture by stealing Native children from their families, forcing them to convert to Christianity, and torturing or killing them if they refused to renounce their community's practices (like not cutting their hair or speaking their own languages). In the United States, the residential school system began with George Washington, reached its peak in the 1960s, and continues to this day. We cannot actually know the full scope of this racialized religious violence, because both the US government and the Roman Catholic Church, administrators of these schools, refuse to make their records of these atrocities public.

Note the dual operation of empire here: both the United States and the Roman Catholic Church continue to assert their sovereignty over Native peoples and continue to rest on the Doctrine of Discovery, by refusing to acknowledge, much less reckon with, their collective genocidal past.

When we say racialized religion has real material consequences, we mean they are matters of life, death, and dignity after death—because, as poet and scholar of Native religions Denise K. Lajimodiere teaches us in *Stringing Rosaries* (2019), Native survivors are still trying to find the discarded remains of their stolen relatives, still trying to find ways to live in the wake of these religio-racial atrocities.

When we say racialized religion works in the service of American empire, we mean that America largely refuses to extend its foundational protections for religious freedom to Native people doing what US imperial Christianity insisted they learn to call "religion." This is still happening. As recently as 1990, the US Supreme Court ruled that constitutional protections for religion did not extend to the Native American Church's practice of ingesting peyote, a controlled substance in most states per the FDA.

This Supreme Court ruling, *Employment Division v. Smith* (1990), led Congress to pass the Religious Freedom Restoration Act (1993) and several others intended to protect minoritized religious communities. But so far the RFRA has been most effectively deployed to protect white Christian business practices, including the right of white evangelical bakers to discriminate against queer people and the right of white evangelical peddlers of pipe cleaners, Hobby Lobby, to circumvent the Affordable Care Act's contraceptive mandate. (More on that in chapter 4.)

Appeals to religious freedom also don't protect Native lands in the United States. Pope Francis might have apologized (in 2023!!!) for the Roman Catholic Church's complicity in Native genocide, but the US is still applying the Doctrine of Discovery in Native land claims. This practice is not unique to the US, either—Australia, New Zealand, Canada, and other settler-colonial states all use and reinterpret the Doctrine of Discovery to maintain and bolster their own specific imperial legacies. Even when military veterans appealed on behalf of Native NODAPL water protectors, insisting water protectors were "not protesting" but "praying," the US federal government allowed the Dakota Access Pipeline to be built through and pollute Native cemeteries. Protectors of Mauna Kea, a mountain sacred to Native Hawaiians, have successfully stalled but not defeated attempts to build a massive, land-destroying Thirty Meter Telescope there. Through these examples and so many others, we see Native people use religion to resist and survive, while American empire uses religion to suppress and disenfranchise Native people.

Perhaps nowhere do we see the ambivalence of racialized religion and white Christian nationalism converge as clearly and offensively as in the case of the so-called QAnon Shaman, a visible and vocal participant in the insurrectionist attack on the US Capitol on January 6, 2021. You might remember the photos of his *Braveheart* face paint, tattoos that (among other jumbled imagery) invoke Norse paganism to champion white supremacy, and horns that are definitely not compensating for anything. While his public presentation is a mélange of cultures and confusion, we cannot dismiss the persistence of Native customs and imagery throughout. He claims a "shamanic" identity rooted in Native practices; those horns mimic Native buffalo headdresses; he called his face paint "war paint" in a 2020 interview with the *Arizona Republic*. (All *we* saw was Messy Man, but that's beside the point.)

He was arrested and (briefly) incarcerated for his actions, upon which his attorney requested—he didn't even have to sue! in this economy!!—that the shaman be served organic produce because of his alleged "shamanic belief system and way of life." Very few Native people receive religious dietary considerations while incarcerated, and this country incarcerates Native men at a rate higher than any other race or ethnicity. But this white man's appropriation of Native customs and practices gave him legal standing to request healthier food than most incarcerated people, much less most incarcerated Native people, have access to, precisely because he laid claim to religious protections under the constitution of a government he had just tried to overthrow.

Once more, with feeling: the US Constitution offers protection for religious practices and beliefs. Minoritized populations, among them Native people living in what's now the United States, seldom receive the benefit of these protections. But a jabroni in jumbled appropriation cosplay can use those same constitutional provisions so frequently denied to Native people to access better treatment while incarcerated by laying claim to Native spirituality.

Remember when we said settler colonialism was not just a strategy of domination, but of replacement? Please note how the American carceral system seems especially willing to protect Native religious freedoms when they are invoked by a non-Native jabroni in incoherent appropriation cosplay. This is, to put it mildly, a stark example of how systems built to uphold white Christian nationalism racialize religion. Native appeals to religious freedom didn't stop the Dakota Access Pipeline, but American religious freedom sure did let a white man in Native drag eat organic produce in prison, showing us in no uncertain terms that the religion America is most likely to protect is the religion done by white Christians.

▪ ▪ ▪

Anti-Black and anti-Native hostility are in no way unique to the United States, of course. Neither are Black and Native organizing and activism rooted in religion. We've shown you how anti-Black and anti-Native attitudes and policies grew out of white Christian colonial expansion across the Atlantic Ocean, and you know that white Christian colonialism shaped—is still shaping—the whole world. We've focused on white Christian nationalism in the United States because the making of race through religion is so clear in this nation's history, and because Americans export specifically American strains of anti-Black and anti-Native hostility through global flows of capital. As we'll discuss in the next chapter, we see these attitudes shaping institutions and systems all over the world, perhaps nowhere as clearly as with sexual and reproductive healthcare policies.

▪▪▪▪▪▪▪▪▪▪

FURTHER READING

James Baldwin, "On Being White . . . and Other Lies," *Essence*, April 1984, and "To Crush the Serpent" (1987) in *The Cross of Redemption: Uncollected Writings*, ed. Randall Kenan (New York: Vintage Books, 2010)

Yvonne Chireau, *Black Magic: Religion and the African American Conjuring Tradition* (Berkeley: University of California Press, 2006)

Roxanne Dunbar-Ortiz, *An Indigenous Peoples' History of the United States* (Boston: Beacon Press, 2014)

Sylvester A. Johnson, *African American Religions, 1500–2000: Colonialism, Democracy, and Freedom* (New York: Cambridge University Press, 2015)

Denise K. Lajimodiere, *Stringing Rosaries: The History, the Unforgivable, and the Healing of Northern Plains American Indian Boarding School Survivors* (Fargo: North Dakota State University Press, 2021)

Kathryn Gin Lum, *Heathen: Religion and Race in American History* (Cambridge, MA: Harvard University Press, 2022)

Judith Weisenfeld, *New World A-Coming: Black Religion and Racial Identity During the Great Migration* (New York: NYU Press, 2019)

FURTHER LISTENING ON KEEPING IT 101

(E103) "Major Religions? Minor Religions? Must We?"
(E205) "Gender, Sexuality, and Religion in What's Now the US"
(E404) "What Are Indigenous Religions? Part 2"

RELIGION IS POLITICS

in which religion cannot be kept out of politics
(and we find rather more religion in our pants
than we'd prefer, to be quite honest)

In the last chapter, we walked you through how America built race—and itself as a nation—out of the raw materials of religion. This is called "white Christian nationalism," and we showed you how it uses religion to protect the interests of those with the most cultural capital and power. We also showed you that minoritized people use religion to argue for and protect their own freedom and humanity.

So, sure, people do political things with religion. But what does it mean to say "Religion is politics"? So glad you asked, friends. In this chapter, we want you to pay attention to the ways that religion infuses how we govern ourselves as a nation—and how religious assumptions undergird nominally secular policies that control our bodies.

■   ■   ■

Race and religion are just a few of the ways humans sort ourselves into hierarchies, unequal ways of being in the world that we learn from and teach to other humans, consciously and unconsciously. As you know, social structures shift over time and place as humans' understanding of the world changes.

There are a few constants, of course. People at the top of social hierarchies reinforce existing systems to maintain access to privilege (material and social advantages) and power. One group of people over-powering and exploiting another group of people to maintain power and privilege is as old as humanity itself. But using a framework of unchanging, essential, inheritable *moral* superiority to fuel and further global domination? This is a modern phenomenon—and precisely the work of racialized religious imperialism.

What we're asking you to pay attention to in this chapter is how race and religion, two modern social constructs directly tied to imperi-alism, build on a third: sexuality. You probably don't need us to tell you that sex as a cluster of practices is older than ancient; after all, none of us would be here without it. But *sexuality* (how, where, why, when, if you want to have sex and with whom) distilling into the central truth about yourself really only takes root in the past two centuries or so—and, as you might guess, is directly tied to race, religion, and empire.

Like race, sexuality can feel inherent, unchangeable. But how we identify (the options we have for describing who, how, when, and if we want sex) and the kinds of sex we think are safe to have, safe to *want*, or admit to wanting? We learn those options, those possibilities, from one another. Race and religion, as you know, shape our understandings of what our bodies mean and what we can, what we *need* to do with them. But wait, there's more! Nationalism—our connection to the idea of a country, a lie we tell on maps and defend with bombs—also affects our understandings of our bodies and selves.

The purpose of this chapter is not to walk you through how we construct sexuality out of religion, race, and nationalism. (We do, of course, construct sexuality out of race, religion, and nationalism, but that's not the point of this chapter.) Rather, we want to show you how nations create contemporary systems, like courts and healthcare. These systems explicitly draw on religious understandings of what bodies are for—that is, the assumption that bodies are primarily if not exclusively designed to make more bodies. People have been doing everything it is possible to do with, to, on, around, through, for, and in bodies for as long as bodies have existed. But we owe the assumption that the most important thing people can do with their bodies is make more bodies—in other words, in case it isn't clear, reproduce moderately within heterosexual cisgender married couples—to white Christian nationalism.

Chapter 1 showed you what to look for if you're looking for how people do religion. This chapter wants you to see how religion works on people and through people, which is to say: systemically. We've been saying all along that religion is what people do. The things people do over and over again? For reasons they might not even be 100 percent clear on? The ways we've been taught to assume the world works, *should* work? Those are systems, built by people and (as James Baldwin reminds us) changeable by people. Those systems people built out of religion? Those are politics.

In this chapter, we're showing you that religion is politics because

- all over the world, religion is about power and power works through systems
- in the US and elsewhere, our political systems emerge from white Christian nationalism—which means church and state have never *really* been separate
- and boy, can you ever see religion working through political systems that govern and police our bodies

Even though Americans of many different religions—including some white Christians—support access to abortion healthcare, the US is still letting a regressive white Christian nationalist minority set sexual healthcare policy for all of us. This is just one of myriad examples of how religion works politically (and politics works through and with religion).

We are once again asking you to focus on the United States for a few reasons. First, the stripping of abortion's constitutionality is so stark an example of white Christian nationalism working systemically to be nearly unbelievable—and yet here we find ourselves, in the year of their Lord 2024, disenfranchised and federally robbed of bodily sovereignty. Second, we really need you to sit with the sharp contradiction between this nation's professed commitment to religious freedom and its permissiveness toward white Christian political domination, especially when it comes to matters of sexuality. Third, the United States wields an outsize and frankly terrifying level of influence and impact on global sexual healthcare policies. And finally, if a post-*Dobbs* (the case that removed constitutional protections for abortion) world has taught us nothing else, it's shown us that you can have absolutely zero interest in religion and still not have sovereignty over your own body because of white Christian nationalist sexual ethics.

The confluence of religion and sexuality in and throughout American politics shows us that there is no such thing as apolitical religion.

Anywhere shaped by white Christian imperialism—which, as we told you in chapter 2, is pretty much everywhere—religion shaped and shapes our systems. Religion is, in short, politics. Which means that no matter how you feel about religion, religion is not done with you.

LEGALLY RELIGIOUS

What does it mean to say that religion is politics, though? We're not just talking about elections and laws. Politics refers to the conditions of possibility created by elections and laws, which regulate other systems like schools, businesses, banks, and healthcare. Heck, even the US Postal Service—the appointed rounds of which cannot allegedly be stayed by snow, rain, heat, or gloom of night—shuts down to observe the birth of the Christ Child. Politics is shorthand for the institutions and systems that shape and govern our lives: where we live, what counts as a family, how our money gets used and why, who can do what to whom in public and get away with it.

When we say religion is politics, we mean white Christian nationalism infuses American

- currency
- classrooms
- calendars
- voting practices
- courtrooms
- (and so much more, but space constraints)

Wait, what?

For real, though. All our currency says "in God we trust"; whose god is that, anyway? Every morning, public school children pledge their allegiance to "one Nation under God"; again, whose god? White Christian nationalism is all over our calendars—stay tuned for the homework at the end of this book to learn more. Did you know that Americans vote on Tuesdays because the Founders assumed everyone would be in church on Sundays and folks might need Mondays to travel to the polls? (And, to add insult to injury, your famously not-Christian authors have both voted in Christian houses of worship.) White Christian nationalism is in our courtrooms: Pagan Megan admits to lowering herself to swear on a Christian Bible to get out of a traffic ticket (look, she was in grad school: poverty > principles).

And all of this is before we get into how hard it is to be elected in this country if you're not a white Christian man. Remember how North Carolina, the state that funded both of our PhDs, tried to exempt itself from the First Amendment in 2013 and officially declare itself a Christian state? North Carolina also tried to use the state's constitution to bar an atheist from serving on Asheville's city council in 2009—article 4, section 8, of the state's constitution disqualifies "any person who shall deny the being of Almighty God" from holding public office. On a national level, nonwhite non-Christian nonmale politicians face everything from daily death threats to discriminatory archaic regulations—such as the one forbidding hats on the floor of Congress, which regressive lawmakers attempted to weaponize to keep Representative Ilhan Omar, among the first Muslim women elected to the House of Representatives, from piously covering her head while doing the job her constituents elected her to do.

Religion, and specifically white Christian nationalism, informs and infuses all of these systems. In this chapter, we're going to focus specifically on legal and juridical systems, because the thing about laws is that they require definitions in order to limit their scope and parameters. As you'll see, the US Constitution protects religion in very specific ways. But in order to protect something, you first have to specify what you're protecting (and what you're not). Definitions are by their nature exclusionary: to say "Religion means XYZ" is also to say "Religion is *not* A through W." And by this point in the book, it should come as no surprise that in the US, "XYZ" usually means white Christianity.

Before we get into the nitty-gritty of American political religions and religious politics, it's important to note that religion doesn't just inform *American* politics or American laws. European Christian imperialism has shaped the whole world in many important ways, but for right now, we want you to pay attention to how countries—including but by no means exclusively the United States—use laws and legal precedents to limit and regulate other systems.

The concept of "law" is an ancient one, obviously. (Code of Hammurabi, anyone?) But the idea that the same law applies in the same way to a group of disparate people called a "nation" (and sometimes an entire empire) is a product of European imperial influence. We're being history nerds and digging our heels in about this because Europe's imperial insistence on legal precedence *really* matters for how it's possible for people to be in the world. Once a law is on the books, that law shapes all subsequent interpretations and enforcements on the matter. Legal precedence works differently at different times in different countries, but the effect of earlier law on all future legal and juridical practices is the same the world over. And sometimes the precedent in question is *very* old indeed, as we'll see with *Dobbs*, the US Supreme Court decision that overturned *Roe v. Wade*.

You know that white Christianity drove European imperialism, so you won't be shocked to hear that white European Christian morals, worldviews, and aesthetics drive much of the world's legal precedents. As in the United States, the global effects of white Christian imperialism are especially visible in legal regulations of sexuality. For example: we see white European Christian sexual ethics at work in India's contemporary regulation of homosexuality, even though India has been its own nation-state since 1947. You know from chapter 2 that Christianity has never been a majority religion in India and that India has never been a majority-white state, so how could white Christianity be shaping subcontinental laws in the twenty-first century?

We bet you can answer this question on your own by now, reader: once again, it's white Christian imperialism. India inherited and adapted its civil and criminal codes from British imperial rule, and the British made homosexuality illegal in British India under article 377 in 1861. Indian law rendered same-sex sexual acts illegal until 2018 (just fifteen years after the United States overturned its own sodomy laws in *Lawrence v. Texas*, which we'll return to in a minute).

This isn't to say that pre-1861 South Asia was a queer-friendly paradise. While Indian gender norms included and still include space for nonbinary genders, this does not negate evidence for precolonial hostility toward same-gender-loving people. But cishet white Christian Protestant Britons *codified* antiqueer hostility, enshrining their particular cishet white Christian values into law, enforcing them in the criminal code, and establishing all manner of decisions based on that code, fundamentally imposing Christian norms on a decidedly non-Christian-majority nation. Even after the formal end of British colonial rule, even in the absence of a white or Christian majority in India, India's laws perpetuated an antiqueer hostility rooted in white European Christian sexual morality.

We've made this brief subcontinental detour to underline that white Christian sexual morality doesn't only shape US law and US culture. For the rest of this chapter, though, we want to focus on why and how the United States came to be so very bad at something it claims to be the best at: that is, keeping religion out of politics. Even in cases that don't explicitly address religious practices or religious freedom, American courts filter their understandings of good, proper, moral sexuality through a white Christian nationalist lens. (Religion and law scholars Janet Jakobsen and Ann Pellegrini have done some great work on this, by the way; check out *Love the Sin* [2004].)

Legal regulation of human sexuality is by no means the only place we see nominally secular systems draw on and perpetuate white Christian nationalism, but they might be the clearest example of religion at work on our bodies. Religion and sexuality have a long constitutional history in the United States, the regulation of which largely focuses on ensuring that Americans have the right sort of sex—which is to say, the kind of sex that produces "good" (that is, properly white, properly Christian) Americans.

Anxieties about the wrong sort of people making more people who would threaten the essential whiteness and Christianity of America have been a driving force in regulating polygamy, interracial marriage, parenthood, fertility, and immigration for the entirety of this nation's history. We see this in state-level anti-miscegenation laws (Oklahoma 1908, Louisiana 1920, Maryland 1935), federal immigration restrictions like the Chinese and Asian Exclusion Acts (1882 and 1924), forced sterilization practices (*Buck v. Bell* 1927), and anti-Native policies like the ones we discussed in chapter 3. Underlying all these regulations—these systems—were anxieties about America becoming something other than a country rooted in properly white Christianity, even when the laws themselves did not explicitly address religion or race.

This might sound confusing, though—aren't the courts supposed to be secular?

Indeed they are, reader! But think back to chapter 1: secularism is not an absence of religion; it's a diffusion of white Christian values and commitments into institutions and systems that are not explicitly religious. So, while Supreme Court rulings on sexuality don't always explicitly *say* they're about religion, the patterns in those decisions tell us something important about what the court (and, by extension, the country) thinks is moral, permissible, *civilized*, for Americans to do with their bodies.

CHURCH AND STATE ARE NOT SEPARATE— THEY'RE NOT EVEN ON A BREAK

You already know that American understandings of race grew out of religion; so, too, did American understandings of sexuality. Just as we see white Christian nationalism govern systems that reinforce and perpetuate racial hierarchies, we see white Christian nationalism inform systems that reinforce and perpetuate sexual hierarchies. These hierarchies intersect, further complicating the ways American polices appropriate behaviors for bodies.

But what about the separation of church and state, we hear you asking? Religion professors in the US get this question a lot, especially during times of religio-political controversy. Bad news, reader. The separation of church and state kind of doesn't exist. It sort of never did? At least not in the way most folks think.

There *are* protections for religion in the US Constitution; it's true. There are maybe not as many protections as you might assume, and they are certainly not as robust as the phrase "separation of church and state" might have led us to believe. (See, we told you belief is a misdirect.) There are, in fact, three protections for religion in the US Constitution.

The only protection for religion in the Constitution proper is Article VI, Clause 3, which forbids the administration of religious tests for anyone seeking to hold political office or access any "public trust" (usually interpreted as natural and cultural resources) in the United States. This roughly means you don't—or shouldn't—have to prove you're any particular religion to receive fair treatment by the US government. Supreme Court Justice Sonia Sotomayor based her dissent to *Trump v. Hawaii* (2018) in part on Article VI, Clause 3, saying that restrictions on travel from Muslim majority countries were a de facto religious test, rendering the so-called Muslim ban unconstitutional.

The remaining—and far more frequently cited—protections for religion in the US Constitution are the very first part of the Bill of Rights, an enumerated list of conditions added to the original Constitution to limit the powers of America's federal government. The First Amendment, as the name suggests, was the first limitation on the government's powers. Its very first clauses require that "Congress shall make no law respecting an establishment of religion, or prohibiting the free exercise thereof." These protections are known as the establishment clause and the free exercise clause.

The establishment clause is at the heart of what most people think "separation of church and state" means. To establish a religion is to put the weight of a country behind that religion—so, no matter what your private religious commitments (or lack thereof) might be, if you live in that country, you have to publicly support the established (favorite) religion. Establishment can look like tax dollars supporting clergy and institutions, or the government mandating public participation in the established religion's holidays. Before the Founders ratified the Constitution, states collected taxes from citizens of all religious backgrounds and directed those funds toward Christian churches. Massachusetts, the last state in the union to disestablish, collected taxpayer funds as late as 1833!

In his 1802 letter to the Danbury Baptist Association, Thomas Jefferson said that the establishment clause built "a wall of separation between Church & State," insisting that Americans' allegiance was to their "social duties" rather than any particular religious organization. The establishment clause forbids the federal government from privileging any one religious institution over other religious institutions or communities. But, in practice, the United States *does* legally and socially establish a preferential option for white Christianity and its practitioners—especially, as we'll discuss in a moment, when it comes to telling Americans what they can and cannot do with their own bodies.

The free exercise clause is the basis for what most Americans mean when they talk about religious freedom—a plain text reading of "Congress shall make no law . . . prohibiting the free exercise [of religion]" *looks like* it means religious people are free to practice according to their best understandings of their private religious commitments. But free exercise is not a get-out-of-jail-free (if you did the crime for religious reasons) card.

For the most part, the free exercise clause protects freedom of religious belief: you are personally free to *believe* whatever you like and the US government cannot penalize you for those beliefs. But—as you remember from chapter 1—religion is about so much more than belief! So, for example, Seventh-day Adventists have always been free to *believe* that they should observe a religious day of rest and reflection on Saturday rather than Sunday, the traditional Christian sabbath. But Seventh-day Adventist Adele Sherbert had to take her case all the way to the US Supreme Court to receive compensation when her employer terminated her for refusing to work on Saturdays (*Sherbert v. Verner*, 1963).

American courts and American laws, shaped by white Christian imperial thinking about religion, really struggle with what religion is when it's not just about belief. Again, this isn't just us quibbling about minutiae. The US Constitution provides specific protections for religion, but laws can't protect what they can't define. We said at the top of this chapter that laws require a definition of religion in order to protect religion, that "religion is XYZ" also means "religion is not A through W." Words and phrases in the Constitution—words like "establishment," for example, or phrases like "free exercise"—don't mean anything on their own. Instead, these concepts come to mean things through the enforcement and adjudication of laws.

For almost a century after the Founders ratified the Constitution, free exercise was widely construed to protect differences in religious practices. That is, until a new kind of white Christianity (Mormonism) tried to practice a very old kind of marriage (polygamy, a form of multiple-partner marriage). The US Supreme Court issued its first definition of religious free exercise in *Reynolds v. United States* (1878), ruling that while Americans were free to *believe* whatever they liked, American criminal and civil laws still pertained to religious practices— even practices with extensive biblical precedent, like polygamy.

Without getting too lost in the weeds of Mormon or American legal history, this means that the Supreme Court's very first definition of free exercise isn't just about religion—it's about sexuality. It's also about race: *Reynolds* condemns the practice of polygamy, religious or otherwise, as "odious among the northern and western nations of Europe, and, until the establishment of the Mormon Church, almost exclusively a feature of the life of Asiatic and of African people." That is, the Supreme Court said in so many words that by using religion to publicly engage in "uncivilized" (that is, allegedly not white, not Western) sexual practices, the nascent Mormon Church forfeited its constitutional religious protections. The first time the US Supreme Court defines free exercise—one of only three constitutional protections for religion, and the only one that pertains to religious communities' practices—it does so in a way that unanimously tells even white

Christians that religious freedom doesn't extend so far as to excuse sexual behaviors it finds *unbecoming* of white Christians.

We know you know by now that legal definitions of religion tend to privilege white Christian ways of being religious. This includes privileging beliefs over practices, but it also means that US courts and laws most often protect religious practices that conform to what they think white Christianity should look like. This includes Supreme Court decisions that insist, for example, that the cross is a broadly *American* rather than exclusively Christian symbol (*American Legion v. American Humanist Association*, 2018).

To protect religious freedom, the Supreme Court needs to define religion. *Reynolds* shows us that even though the idea of religion grows out of white Christianity, American institutions do not necessarily protect the practices of all white Christians. It's harder to be whiter than Joseph Smith and his band of Merry Men, but the Supreme Court ruled that polygamy was a barbaric (which is to say, unworthy of white Christians) practice. The unspoken but clearly expressed fear was that the nascent Church of Jesus Christ of Latter-day Saints would use polygamy to outpopulate and outnumber "real" Americans, fundamentally shifting the country away from its white Christian nationalist roots.

As with British and later Indian regulation of homosexuality in South Asia, the US Supreme Court's rulings regarding legal sexual practices follow white Christian sexuality morality. The Supreme Court codifies white Christian sexual morality and its cishet moderately procreative compulsory heterosexuality: the conviction that the primary if not exclusive purpose of human bodies is making more humans, and that only the right sort of humans should be permitted to make more humans. *Reynolds* is the first but by no means the last Supreme Court decision that limits "real" religion—that is, practices worthy of legal protection—to white Christian nationalist notions of acceptable sexuality.

WHITE CHRISTIAN NATIONALISM IN YOUR UTERUS

Decisions like *Reynolds* and the other cases discussed in this chapter show us America's position on permissible sexual behaviors—and how that position is often shaped by white Christian nationalist assumptions about what is moral for bodies to do (or have done to them). Obviously individual Americans hold, and always have held, myriad opinions about what sorts of things are okay to do with which sorts of bodies. But the Supreme Court is the final word on the constitutionality of these matters.

Supreme Court decisions about sexuality do not always explicitly reference religion; in fact, most of the major twentieth-century decisions about sexuality make no reference to religion at all! But, whether the court talks about religion or not, we need you to see white Christian nationalism lurking in the floorboards of that courtroom. Religion was certainly lurking on June 24, 2022, when the *Dobbs* decision voided federal protections for abortion access, thereby robbing all Americans of their bodily autonomy and surrendering our country to a fringe extremist interpretation of white Christian nationalist sexual ethics.

This isn't to say that the United States or its Supreme Court always and everywhere rules in ways that uphold white Christian nationalist sexual morality. Indeed, for much of the late twentieth and early twenty-first century, the court moved in more progressive directions with regard to sexuality. So how did we get here?

To understand our current religious political moment, we need to do a quick bit of history—if for no other reason than to show how Americans' access to abortion became a matter of national debate fifty years after *Roe v. Wade* should have secured pregnable people's abortion access in the US in perpetuity.

In the twentieth and early twenty-first century, the US Supreme Court handed down a cluster of decisions that prioritized due process (equal treatment under the law) and an individual's right to privacy.

Unlike in *Reynolds*, which focused on securing the federal government's dominion over citizen's bodies, these decisions prioritized individuals' privacy and equality. The cases addressed laws and policies designed to keep the "wrong" sort of people from making the "wrong" sort of Americans, and to prevent anyone from having the kinds of sex that can't make more Americans. (Which is to say, laws and policies that kept Americans from deciding when or if they wanted to be pregnant, whom they can marry, and with whom they can have nonreproductive sex in private.) Significant milestones on this due process and individual privacy timeline include:

- the right to use contraceptives—*Griswold v. CT* (1965) for married couples, *Eisenstadt v. Baird* (1972) for single people
- the right to marry the person of your choosing regardless of race—*Loving v. Virginia* (1968)
- the right to terminate a pregnancy—*Roe v. Wade* (1973)
- the right to have consensual sex that can't result in pregnancy in your own home—*Lawrence v. Texas* (2003)
- the right to marry the person of your choosing regardless of gender—*Obergefell v. Hodges* (2015)

A few important notes on these cases, before we move on. First, while none of them were, on their faces, about religion, *all* of them addressed white Christian nationalist sexual morals that states codified into law. Second—believe it or not—most of these were not contentious decisions! The Supreme Court decision for *Griswold* was 7–2, and even though he dissented, Justice Potter Stewart (whom you might remember from his inability to define pornography, but his ability to recognize it on sight) called Connecticut's anti-contraception statute "uncommonly silly." *Loving v. Virginia* was a unanimous decision, and while *Roe v. Wade* was 7–2 rather than unanimous, none of the dissenting judges even bothered to write a formal dissent.

Finally and most importantly, Americans secured all these rights *not* on the basis of bodily sovereignty or autonomy, but on the basis of privacy and equal treatment under the law. The Supreme Court told Americans that they deserved to be treated equally, and while the Constitution didn't explicitly protect their privacy, there was enough to suggest they probably also deserved privacy from state interventions into sexual practices. This is very much not the same thing as the Supreme Court telling Americans the Constitution protects their rights to control their own bodies. In fact, no Supreme Court decision has ever ruled that Americans have the right to control their own bodies.

That said, abortion in particular was not always such a powder keg of a religious or political issue for most Americans. Which can be hard to fathom in the US's current political moment, we know. But it really wasn't! In fact, abortion has never been a religion on one side/bodily sovereignty on the other debate. Before *Roe*, mainstream Protestants mostly thought of the prohibition against abortion as a strictly Catholic issue, and there have always been Christians—even Catholics—who advocate for abortion access as a fundamental human right. (Patricia Miller's *Good Catholics* [2015] is a great introduction to this complicated moment in American religious history.) It's not until after 1973, following *Roe*, that we see a confederation of ultra-conservative mostly white mostly Christian mostly men consolidate into the religious political powerhouse that would become the New Christian Right and the so-called Moral Majority.

For the next half-century, these hateful pundits and their descendants lobbied relentlessly to end abortion access, claiming that their narrow, regressive understanding of human sexuality was the true and only manifestation of American values. As American religious historian Gil Frank has argued, conservatives started doubling down on controlling sexuality starting in the 1970s, when the blatant racism of their platform in the 1950s and 1960s became increasingly less politically expedient on a national level.

(Remember when blatant racism was detrimental to conservative political campaigns? For that matter, remember when George Washington said America is a country that "to bigotry gives no sanction, to persecution no assistance"? Yeah, us too. Oh well.)

In 2022, the anti-abortion lobby finally succeeded: in *Dobbs v. Jackson Women's Health Organization*, five mostly white, mostly male, exclusively Christian (and mostly Catholic) justices robbed an entire nation of their heretofore constitutional right to terminate a pregnancy.

We have been saying that law is important not only for its immediate effects but also for the persistence of precedent. White Catholic justice Samuel Alito's majority opinion for *Dobbs* draws on an English legal religious penalty from, we're not even kidding, the freaking *twelfth* century. (Alito also played fast and loose with the precedent he cited: the original text says a woman who ends the life of a "quick," or demonstrably alive, child should "do penance"—which is to say, religiously repent. Alito's citation omits the "penance" part to equate abortion with murder and suggest erroneously that abortion was a criminal act in medieval England.) The precedent for this twenty-first-century decision that disenfranchises all Americans by robbing them of their bodily sovereignty is older than the concepts of whiteness, religion, and the United States itself.

This would have been bad enough, but in his concurrence, Black Catholic credibly accused sexual predator Justice Clarence Thomas signaled his intention to overturn the right to marriage regardless of gender (*Obergefell*), the right to have consensual sex in your own home regardless of gender (*Lawrence*), and the right to use contraception (*Griswold*). The right to marriage regardless of race (*Loving*) is conspicuously absent from this list, which might or might not have something to do with Justice Thomas's own marriage to a rabidly anti-abortion and notoriously white woman (herself connected to numerous groups that lobbied to overturn *Roe*).

It's important to note that the *Dobbs* decision is not, on its face, about religion. As with *Obergefell*, *Lawrence*, *Roe*, *Loving*, and *Griswold*, the Supreme Court based their majority opinion on the individual's right to privacy (or lack thereof) and to due process, equal treatment under the laws. But, in action, *Dobbs* further codifies white Christian nationalist sexual morality by making it harder for people to have sex without making more people.

Indeed, humanity—who is a person and who is not, when a person becomes a person—is at the heart of this ruling, even though the majority opinion fails to weigh in on the issue of personhood directly. And it is precisely the issue of personhood that makes *Dobbs* such a flagrant violation of both the free exercise and establishment clauses of the First Amendment.

The very first sentences of the *Dobbs* decision allow that there is no religious consensus on when or if a fetus is a person. At the same time, in its effects *Dobbs* erases the complexity of religious personhood debates, especially within Judaism and Islam, by privileging white Christian nationalist perspectives on abortion. While *Dobbs* offers no comment on "fetal personhood," by headfaking at the concept's legitimacy, the precedent set by this case opens the floodgates for states to implement laws that codify white Christian nationalist arguments that humanity begins at conception. (See, for example, the so-called heartbeat laws that grant protections to non-sentient nonviable clumps of cells—sometimes forfeiting the life of the parent to privilege that cell clump's potential viability.)

The American debate about bodily autonomy is not as straightforward as religion on one side and abortion on the other. Many religious communities, including Jewish, Muslim, as well as some Christian communities, support and even celebrate abortion as a fundamental human right. Though they differ in important ways, both Judaism and Islam prioritize the life of the parent in considering the morality of terminating a pregnancy. Islamic law is on the side of mercy, particularly toward the life of the parent; indeed, there is *no* Muslim-majority country with abortion regulations as restrictive as those of some states in the post-*Dobbs* United States. And Jewish law goes so far as to *require* abortion in cases when a pregnancy endangers the parent's life. There is, in short, no one religious position on the morality of abortion; many religious communities understand abortion as a moral and sometimes even necessary medical intervention.

But—as we saw with *Reynolds v. US* and Mormonism in this chapter and with *Employment v. Smith* and Native religions in chapter 3—the Supreme Court tends to define "religious freedom" in terms that privilege white Christian nationalism rather than protect the complex and multiple perspectives of American religious communities. This is certainly the case with *Dobbs*, and the sitting Supreme Court justices have signaled their intention to continue establishing white Christianity as the de facto religion of the United States while undermining our constitutional commitment to free exercise.

WHITE CHRISTIAN NATIONALISM IN THE WHOLE WORLD'S UTERUSES

Even if you are not American, even if you do not give a care about the United States (and, frankly, who could blame you?), these legal precedents still have an impact on you. Because of the scope of America's global economic and military influence, how the United States understands and polices human sexuality has repercussions far beyond our borders.

The US government is the world's leading source of international aid. Global organizations that address humanitarian crises are often dependent upon American funding to operate. Without that money, some of the poorest and most vulnerable people in the world cannot, do not, survive. That funding is not free—it comes with restrictions set by the United States. Those restrictions mirror (and in some cases massively surpass) American domestic regulations, especially when it comes to sexuality. This is yet another place where we see American white Christian nationalism affect the whole world.

The so-called Mexico City policy is just one example of the international harm caused by the politics of American white Christian nationalism. The Mexico City policy, also known as the "global gag rule," denies funding to humanitarian organizations that so much as mention abortion. When President Ronald Reagan passed the global gag rule in 1984, this policy only pertained to family planning and sexual health organizations—organizations that provide child or parental healthcare, but also organizations that were providing HIV prevention education and treatment during the height of the global AIDS crisis. This means nongovernmental organizations whose only mission was to hand out condoms to prevent the spread of HIV/AIDS could lose their funding and cease to exist just for mentioning that abortion exists. They didn't need to provide abortions or even recommend that someone have one; speaking the word "abortion" was enough to kill US support altogether.

The US massively expanded the global gag rule in 2017; healthcare advocates called this expansion the "global gag rule on steroids." Under this version of the Mexico City policy, *any* NGO—from preventing HIV/AIDS to stopping the spread of malaria to ensuring access to clean drinking water—could lose its funding for mentioning abortion.

This isn't just about freedom of speech (which, to be fair, the First Amendment only applies to Americans anyway). Imagine you're a woman in India seeking treatment for your malaria. The NGO handing out malaria pills asks you if you've had any significant surgical procedures. Abortion is legal in India; you tell your NGO healthcare provider that you had one last year. Your healthcare provider now faces a choice: she can end the conversation and keep her organization's funding intact, or she can treat you based on her knowledge of your medical history. She cannot do both.

This paradox is where we see America's white Christian nationalism doing imperialism across the globe. Because America is the world's primary source of humanitarian aid—because we have the most money and the most guns and bombs—American politicians get to set international policy. And their policies reflect white Christian nationalist priorities about and limitations on acceptable sexuality, regardless of how religious people in non-American countries might feel about the morality of, for example, abortion.

After 2017, the global gag rule affected over seventy countries and $12 billion in international aid. Even after its contraction in January 2021, the US has refused to formally repeal the global gag rule, meaning future presidents can reinstate this harmful policy at will. American white Christian nationalism and its obsession with our bodies lives to fight another day.

This chapter isn't intended as a comprehensive outline of the intricacies of religious arguments for or against abortion. Rather, we hope you've seen how nominally secular systems like laws and courts codify white Christian nationalism even in countries whose founding documents supposedly enshrine religious freedom and disestablishment. For this and many related reasons, American religious historian Sylvester Johnson argues that the United States might not be a white Christian *state*—a country that formally and explicitly requires whiteness and Christianity for full citizenship and political enfranchisement—but it is demonstrably a Christian *nation*, a country that in practice privileges whiteness and codes specific Christian commitments and worldviews as good old American values. Let's take that a step further: policies like the global gag order show us that America is trying to remake the whole world in its prudish white Christian image. It's updated, it's Americanized, but it is still guys with pens using systems they built to privilege their ideas, bodies, power, and religion enacting all that on the rest of the world.

Or, to put it plainly: religion is politics (and vice versa, with emphasis on the vice).

▪ ▪ ▪

In our next and final chapter, we'll show you how moving through the world requires us to participate in systems that perpetuate religious discrimination and intolerance—even when we are ourselves personally committed to religious diversity and freedom. Airports are, in our opinion, a perfect place to see how religion is about more than belief, how religion creates and maintains borders, how race and religion cocreate each other, and how religion is never operating apolitically.

▪▪▪▪▪▪▪▪▪▪▪

FURTHER READING

Zahra Ayubi, "There Is No One Islamic Interpretation on Ethics of Abortion, but the Belief in God's Mercy and Compassion Is a Crucial Part of Any Consideration," *The Conversation*, July 8, 2022

Gillian Frank, "The Deep Ties Between the Catholic Anti-Abortion Movement and Racial Segregation," *Jezebel*, January 22, 2019

Megan Goodwin, *Abusing Religion: Literary Persecution, Sex Scandals, and American Minority Religions* (New Brunswick, NJ: Rutgers University Press, 2020)

Janet R. Jakobsen and Ann Pellegrini, *Love the Sin: Sexual Regulation and the Limits of Religious Tolerance* (New York: NYU Press, 2003)

Sajida Jalalzai, "Please Stop Using Islam to Critique the Abortion Ban: It Only Excuses the Very Christian, Very White Roots of Anti-Choice Movements," *Religion Dispatches*, September 3, 2021

Patricia Miller, *Good Catholics: The Battle over Abortion in the Catholic Church* (Berkeley: University of California Press, 2015)

Danya Ruttenberg, "My Religion Makes Me Pro-Abortion," *The Atlantic*, June 14, 2022

FURTHER LISTENING ON KEEPING IT 101

(E201) "Race, Gender, and Sexuality: What's Religion Got to Do with 'Em?"

(SGS2) "Religious Nationalism"

(E502) "INCORRECT: Reproductive Healthcare"

RELIGION IS A FLIGHT RISK

*in which we take you to the airport to show you
just a few of the many ways religion is not
done with you and leave you there*

We have been saying that religion is what people do, and we hope by now you've learned the drill: "people" means systems, institutions, regimes of power. We've said that religion helps structure laws, policies, customs, expectations, institutions, and possibilities all over the world. We've seen how systems work: we imagined how social norms, rituals, cultures, and communities can be seen through Red Sox nation; we thought about how religions were invented and reified during colonization through the cunning use of maps; we chatted about how we cannot and should never think about race without thinking about religion, nor religion without thinking race; and you just heard about how religion is politics via the regulation of sexuality. *Systems* have been the backbone of this book, for good reason. All the stuff of systems—those religion-shaped laws, policies, expectations, institutions, customs, and possibilities—all land, with great force, upon our racialized, sexualized, nationalized bodies.

This means religion is a crucial part of how we understand who we are and how we can or should be in the world. However you feel about religion, whether *a* religion or *any* religion is important in your life, even if you've never uttered a prayer or wondered about what happens when we die:

Religion is not done with you.

Yes, *you*.

Take a trip with us, if you will, to see this bold claim in real life—in a magical, strange place where everything we've explained so far collides. Where's that, you ask? Oh, just your run-of-the-mill airport.

In concluding this book, we show you that:

- religion shapes airports and our experiences of them
- security, surveillance, and "If You See Something, Say Something" all assume religion
- America's white Christian nationalist understanding of religion, especially after 9/11, changes the how whole world identifies and polices security threats

The airport is a perfect place to see how religion—not belief, not practice, not what you as an individual choose to do—really is not done with you.

Pack your bags and join us, won't you?

PREFLIGHT CHECK-IN

It's a hackneyed joke to complain about the airport. Very Jerry Seinfeld circa 1992 asking, "What's the *deal* with airports?" But the joke's on you, nerds. Because we are not letting it go and, in fact, we have arrived here, our almost-final destination.

To board a plane—a privilege you've paid mightily for, economically, temporally, and with the cost of surveillance—demands interactions with the state that inherently assume violence, given the omnipresence of checkpoints, guns, tasers, handcuffs, and airport jails.

The airport is an enchanted, curséd land: out of time, space, and place, where tax-free booze and cigarettes entice, fries can be had at any hour of the day, gates need to be checked repeatedly, security measures make everyone's blood pressure *just high enough* to cultivate that airport-specific anxiety, and religion is everywhere all at once. We don't just mean that you can see religion at the airport, like nondenominational prayer rooms, or the ways that being in the air in a metal tube at hundreds of miles an hour can make many agnostics and mostly secular folks dive into prayerful, mindful, hopeful, or even superstitious thinking. We could mean the ads for various churches in airports, the Disney families some thirty strong all in matching garb, or the travelers awaiting departure for any number of other, non-Mouse-affiliated pilgrimage sites. We could also mention how meditation and mindfulness show up, the growing "wellness" stations in and around concourses, and all the self-help books at the airport kiosks. But we don't. Because we think that the only real example to help us show you the nitty-gritty of how religion is not done with us is to talk (again) about how religion gets racialized.

At the contemporary airport? Religion is racialized. (You'll remember from previous chapters: the racialization of religion is the process through which a religion is linked entirely to one ethnic, racial, or linguistic group, and its assumed adherents are assigned specific, immutable, inheritable characteristics.) Security states surveil and profile people through a racialized religious lens. These assumptions about belief, practice, and voluntarism (which you'll remember from the first chapter; we'll circle back below) make people miss flights, miss medication, miss their families, and sometimes go missing themselves.

So in this chapter, we are definitely summoning Seinfeld and asking: What's the deal with airports? We're answering it not with silly little jokes about peanuts, but by showing you how religion shows up there—often against our wills. Because, hackneyed joke or not, the airport shows us almost everything we've talked about in this book so far in one place.

ARRIVALS

On that note, play along with us, will you? Be with us in this anxiety-laden space. Look around. Really look around: What do you see as you stand with us in line for security at the airport? Do you see religion? Where?

Religion is definitely in line for security all the time—and, perhaps not surprisingly, not in particularly positive ways. This is a real story, this next bit; it happened to Ilyse in early 2018.

She's coming home from Chicago, if memory serves. We're not even through security when religion hits Ilyse square in the chest. Uh, literally. See, she was nursing her youngest at the time, and schlepping a breast pump across the country. On the way home, she was packing liquid gold (aka expressed breast milk), which the TSA allows on flights in larger quantities than shampoo or lotion or Vaseline. But "TSA officers may need to test the liquids for explosives or concealed prohibited items," the rule says. Ilyse, a mostly-rule-follower and definitely-does-not-mess-with-cops kind of gal informs the TSA at the start that she's carrying a breast pump and expressed breast milk in excess of 3.4 ounces, as the website instructed her to do to avoid a random test.

Despite following the TSA's own instructions to the letter, Ilyse is quickly taken aside. Standing with her is an elderly Sikh man, who has been randomly selected for screening; "randomly selected," he says, just like every time he travels. The TSA agent informs Ilyse that her milk needs "testing," and she watches, in the pain only nursing parents understand, as the officers open six Medela five-ounce bottles one by one, insert litmus strips using gloved hands, kind of spill one bottle a bit, then leave the bottles open and out of the specifically-bought-for-this ice pack container.

While her milk is being tested, while she's watching others get patted down but sent on their way, while she and the Sikh uncle are left stranded and waiting, while their bags are systematically and thoroughly unpacked, undone, rummaged through—right then, when her bags are being searched and she catches the side-eye from the searcher, Ilyse realizes she has left a Persian-language book in her backpack. Rookie mistake.

The questions start: Why do you have this milk? Why do you have this book? What language is this? Where do you work, again? She's not proud of it, but Ilyse—watching the time tick, watching the milk just be *open outside in the airport*, with those litmus strips hanging out, with her bags and nursing and pumping paraphernalia and "controversial" books just strewn about—hits the limit of frustration. She is flustered. She is upset. She is anxious. She has that "I'm from New Jersey and I both can and will fight you" scowl going on. She is basically about to cry. (Ilyse usually cries about once a decade.)

And the Sikh uncle, who is also still waiting, puts his arm around her and says: This is the hardest part, dear, but it'll be over soon.

This is the moment at which Ilyse understands: religion is at the airport. In the shared exchange between strangers, yes, but also in this kind man's patient, practiced, ritualized understanding of how degrading this experience was for both of them.

She's feeling deeply embarrassed that a Sikh man—salt-and-pepper beard tucked neatly, gray turban folded perfectly—was comforting *her* while simultaneously experiencing systemic surveillance and religio-racism. He had experienced it *enough* to be able to offer comfort. Felt empathetic *enough* to know how long it would take—how long it took when his daughter's milk had been searched and tested and ultimately ruined because, truly, who wants to feed their infant milk that has had random hands in it?

Religion at the airport for Ilyse is almost always about surveillance, Islamophobia, and profiling. It was evident in the association of the Persian-language book with a raised eyebrow and additional questions, and in the identity of her long-standing linemate, a Sikh man who'd been experiencing this level of intense airport scrutiny since, oh, roughly September 2001.

Megan only started recognizing these patterns of systemic religious racism in grad school—as we've discussed, systems work really hard to get you to ignore them, and it's definitely possible to earn multiple degrees in American religions without proving you can think critically about race. Megan is also autistic, which means she's frequently surprised when people are awful. (This is very inconvenient, as many people are often awful. Megan is surprised every time. It's exhausting.) So when she rolled her eyes and snarked at the TSA yet again "randomly screening" a brown bearded man who was waiting to board her flight, she was genuinely shocked to hear her blonde white lady seatmate mumble gravely, "Yeah, you can't be too careful." Apparently we *don't* all know that the TSA and American security theater aren't about being careful—they're about reminding all of us who the United States marks as safe, as free to move around the world, as human.

For anyone born in the twenty-first century, and, frankly, even for those of us who are older, it can be hard to picture airports being the groovy carefree spaces you see in *Mad Men* and other nostalgic media. How did we get here? Look, it's a cliché for a reason: 9/11 changed everything.

9/11 CHANGED EVERYTHING (FOR THE US, WHO THEN CHANGED EVERYBODY ELSE)

September 11, 2001, is one of those global cultural inflection points not, sadly, because of the loss of life on its own, or the loss of life that followed global war in its wake. 9/11 is one of those watershed moments because of how radically the world changed—how informal mores became formal policies, how quickly laws and customs shifted, how immediately American definitions of security, surveillance, and threat became global norms—almost overnight.

9/11 was an attack immediately framed and understood in terms of religion. And, yes, we cannot and would never pretend that a particularly violent and extremist (and absolutely fringe) gloss of Islam didn't influence and inspire the nineteen men who planned and carried out those terrible hijackings. It did. And part of our jobs as scholars of religion is to acknowledge the complexity and contradictions inherent in being human. Muslims, who are people, are capable of extraordinary beauty as well as unimaginable violence, like all people.

Religious extremism and religious extremists are part of the religion people do. We would never discount that harm or that devastation. But, in the wake of 9/11, the United States has forced the whole world into a *response* to one particular type of racialized religious extremism massively out of proportion to the threat posed *by* the perpetrators of that violence. (As sociologist Charlie Kurzman reminds us in *The Missing Martyrs* [2018]: there is absolutely a small group of Muslims who do terrorism, but, numbers-wise, almost no Muslims are terrorists.)

The men who planned, executed, and funded the 9/11 terrorist attacks were Muslim. So were thousands of scholars, activists, and regular people who condemned and mourned that attack (to say nothing of the Muslim victims themselves). Muslims are by far the most common victims of Islamic terrorism. Knowing that religion is what people do means we have to pay attention to all the ways people use religion, and all the ways people use religion to harm and help one another.

But the United States and its TSA aren't interested in this kind of complexity. Rather, the US has used the tragedy of 9/11 to justify decades of religio-racist policies and practices—and forcibly export those policies and practices all over the world. By this point in the book, you know that racism and religious intolerance far predate 2001, but the state of airports in the twenty-first century takes this hate to new heights and destinations.

Let's see what we can see about this system of racialized religion and say something about its pernicious presence in the airport (and frankly beyond).

SEE SOMETHING, SAY SOMETHING

After 9/11, we—Americans, absolutely, but also Europeans and later folks around the world (especially in Muslim-minority places, like China and India)—were asked to look more closely. To think more critically, more suspiciously about our neighbors. The threat of terrorism, after all, is the threat of the enemy hiding in plain sight. It is, as Mahmood Mamdani has argued, a new version of the Cold War–era spy, and renews those energies and fears, training them on a new object and imagining Muslims as loyal to Islam rather than country. The threat of terrorism also allows for permanent surveillance of Muslims, even without strong evidence that those communities are uniquely or earnestly invested in such ideologies, as scholars including Deepa Kumar, Arun Kundnani, Saher Selod, and Todd Green have argued.

And yet, globally, we have been trained to look at the behaviors of our neighbors, to notice their subtle body movements on the train, to take our shoes off and carry teeny-tiny shampoos in airports because of the *threat* (imagined or real) of *religious* violence. What exactly do officials hope we see? What exactly are we looking for?

The thing about airports is there's a lot to look at: Free WiFi that isn't really free. Children on those weird, brilliant leashes. Couples about to fight. Celebrity chefs hocking tacos or burgers or taco-burgers. Those really well-dressed international flyers who must have secrets about getting their feet and legs not to swell, because sweatpants are all that's left for us mere mortals.

Wherever you are in the world, there's also usually a recorded voice telling you not to leave your bag unattended, not to accept a bag from a stranger, and always, always to say something if you see something. Did you know that "If You See Something, Say Something" is a registered trademark of the US Department of Homeland Security? It's clever. It's pithy. It's owned and licensed and trademarked and therefore, one assumes, an *asset* to be protected. Someone is profiting off of our collective fear and vigilance. (While we love American ingenuity, truth be told, Ilyse is partial to the UK's cognate campaign "See It, Say It, Sorted," run by the British Transport Police, because it reassures the listener that reporting will fix the problem, encouraging its listeners across modes of transit not only to be vigilant, but to *believe* that vigilance accomplishes something.)

We both travel a lot for work, admittedly, so we hear these kinds of phrases often. Frequently enough that they have *nearly* faded into the background—they are just part of the soundscape of using trains, planes, and hired automobiles. We travel a lot, but have rarely needed to say something, except maybe "Do you need help?" to random moms with their arms full, because that's the kind of world we'd love to live in. But we know that the seeing and saying something—that being told to see it, say it, and let the officials sort it—are actually ways to think about religion not being done with us.

The Department of Homeland Security didn't trademark "If You See Something, Say Something" because they want us to be on the lookout for slower-moving elders who could use *just a minute* (and a bit of grace) at the conveyor belt or parents on the fourth hour of a delay who could use a drink . . . we mean a hand.

Now, we personally see and also say that the various dads scrolling on their phones while their kids run rampant deserve side-eye with extreme prejudice. The witless, uninvolved father at the airport is a threat to his partner's sanity and (statistically) maybe their safety. But we know from being socialized, from living in the world, and from paying attention that this is not the threat governments, transit authorities, and security wants us to report.

We know that the things we're being asked to see and say something about are suspicious characters, not just entitled manchildren. But we also know that we are not being told what constitutes a suspicious character—just that we should always be on high alert lest we see one. We know that we are being asked to see something and say something because *all of us* are meant to be part of the surveillance team, the police force that is omnipresent.

Suspicious characters, we're taught both explicitly and implicitly, are those who *might* do terrorism. That means that what we should be looking out for and what we are meant to say something about are not banal acts of violence and harm—nothing like, say, intimate partner violence or trafficking. That inattentive dad we side-eyed before could easily also be an angry, screaming dad, but that's not the behavior "See It, Say It, Sorted" is asking us to surveil. We are being asked—as a global community—to be on the constant lookout for folks who fit into stereotypes about the kinds of bad guys that do terrorism that hurts all of us, not just one or two of us, and not privately. Bluntly? In a world steeped in both white supremacy and post-9/11 anti-Muslim hostility, the thing we are meant to see and say something about is Blackness, brownness, and Muslimness, because those are the particular threats these systems understand, recognize as threatening, and report.

This isn't just our observation, of course. As Saher Selod in *Forever Suspect* (2018) and Christine Schenk, Banu Gökarıksel, and Negar Behzadi in "Security, Violence, and Mobility" (2022) prove, law enforcement tells us that suspicious characters are brown and Black men, as well as hijab-wearing Muslim women. We know that men wearing turbans, who are typically (though not exclusively) Sikh, are routinely subject not just to the TSA's surveillance, searches, and slow lines, but also to the stares—the sanctioned stares—of people who think they see something and are parsing whether they need to say something.

Anti-Sikh violence in the US and Europe tends to be based in Islamophobia, not anti-Sikh hostility. Let's say that again, because maybe it seems confusing: anti-Muslim hostility makes it hard for Sikh men who wear turbans and have beards to move through the airport easily, without stigma, without surveillance.

And that, dear readers, is the racialization of religion yet again.

When we see—are trained to see, are urged by those in power to see—people who look a certain way as a specifically *religious* threat? That is religio-racism. In the wake of 9/11, the US security state has trained all of us to *see* brownness, beards, head coverings and *say* "Muslim terrorist." We see someone who we've been trained to see as Muslim and assume they are a threat.

Obviously this endangers Muslims trying to move through the world, and especially through an airport. But this kind of religio-racism doesn't just harm Muslims. Because Sikh men are also often brown, often bearded, often turbaned, the TSA often reads them as "Muslim terrorist." (Why do you think that Sikh man was pulled off to be randomly screened with Ilyse's sus breast milk?) Racialization collapses all Muslims and Sikhs into a big category of "problem." Which means state-sponsored Islamophobia targets not just Muslims—though that would be bad enough, especially in a country that prides itself on religious freedom and tolerance—but anyone we've told ourselves *looks* Muslim. The post-9/11 powers that be teach us: See a (potential) Muslim? Report a threat.

What we're trained to see isn't just about appearances. It can also be words we read, like names.

DEPLANING: WHEN OPTING OUT ISN'T AN OPTION

There's an Egyptian American comedian named Ahmed Ahmed who, in 2005, just four years after 9/11 and three years into the war on terror, founded a comedy tour called Axis of Evil. Our younger readers may not know that "axis of evil" is what then-president George W. Bush called Iran, Iraq, and North Korea in his State of the Union address in January 2002; the phrase was repeated ad nauseam and became common parlance as the US, under Bush's leadership, invaded Iraq and later Afghanistan.

The Axis of Evil Comedy Tour featured a core group of comedians with Middle Eastern heritage and featured special guests whose backgrounds were Korean, Middle Eastern, and Cuban—identities marked by racialized (and state-sanctioned) prejudice. The tour and its comedians focused on the post-9/11 experiences of being Arab, Middle Eastern, Asian, Muslim, and Latinx, and they often discussed using comedy as a weapon of mass destruction. (We stan punny comics who use killjoy attitudes to lampoon the horrors of living in a destructive world that specifically seeks to destroy *them*.)

One of Ahmed Ahmed's bits is about one of the many times he was detained for being brown, Middle Eastern, or sharing a name with one of Osama bin Laden's colleagues (minions? bros?). He quips: "My name is Ahmed Ahmed and I can't even fly a kite these days. I'm on, like, nineteen lists." He goes on to talk about how he got thrown in the "brown room," which is for "Middle Easterners, Arabs, Muslims—there was a white guy with a tan in the brown room."

A man named Ahmed Ahmed cannot be anything but "Arab/ Middle Eastern/Muslim" at the airport, a slippery term that scholar Nadine Naber coins in "Look, Muhammad the Terrorist Is Coming!" (2008). The slashes she uses helps us visualize the interchangeable way these distinct ideas—geographic (and multiethnic, multireligious), ethnic (but still multireligious), and religious (but global and multira- cial, multiethnic, multilingual)—get thrown together, homogenized, *racialized* into one thing, despite all this obvious internal diversity and plurality. Ahmed's actual identity, who he thinks he is, how he lives in the world, the religion he does or does not do, has little to do with how he is seen at the airport. At the airport, he is on, "like, nineteen lists" and in and out of the "brown room" regardless of what he does, who he is, how he sees himself, or what he believes.

We are quick to talk about Islamophobia here, and that is abso- lutely true. But it is important to remind you that Islamophobia isn't always about *Islam*: Ahmed is not being detained because of some deeply reasoned theological argument. (FTR, dear nerds, that too would be horrifically inappropriate and bullshit.) The TSA looks at Ahmed Ahmed's passport, sees a Muslim name, and says he's a threat. Ahmed may (or may not) be a practicing Muslim. There is literally no way for the TSA agent to know if he is a devout Muslim, if he is an avowed atheist, if he is another religion altogether. Spoiler: there are many Middle Easterners and Arabs who are not Muslim. These are not the same things. But even if he *were* Muslim, the US Supreme Court has already said that the government and law cannot assess how someone thinks or feels about their religion (*Burwell v. Hobby Lobby Stores*, 2014).

That said, even *if* he were Muslim and even *if* his devotion to Islam could be proven, what the hell does that have to do with terrorism? Wait, wait, don't tell us: Islam has been racialized. So, actually, all the system needs to know—or suspect—is that a person is Muslim to make assumptions about that person's relationship to terror.

The thing the TSA does know is that he *looks* brown—they saw that and said something—and his *name* seems Muslim. (Ahmed is one of the names of Muhammad and an incredibly common name in the Middle East but also South Asia, North America, and in parts of Europe.) And that, post-9/11, is enough to trigger agents, police, investigation, maybe even detention.

We hope in the twenty-first century of America's Lord that we can see racial profiling as problematic; that we can hear how assuming one's religion and predicting that means danger is racist and troubling.

But this experience of power, racism, and American religious intolerance is not the only consequence. The way security functions at the airport? It fundamentally affects an American man named Ahmed Ahmed's First Amendment rights.

In fact, assuming Ahmed Ahmed's religion based on his name or appearance means that Ahmed Ahmed sort of has no real First Amendment rights at all (how, you ask? We'll get there in just a sec).

If he were Muslim, he would have no right to insist that his Islam is not violent, terroristic, problematic—that his practices should be honored and protected. If he were born Muslim and wanted to convert to another religion? No real right to that, since his name indicates *something else*. And if he were an atheist walking around with *that name?* No real right to disavow all religion, either. Ahmed's experience at the airport is one of being seen, having something said, and experiencing what it feels like to be an assumed threat—where those assumptions lead to embarrassment, missed flights, and detention. (And in some cases far worse.)

We tend to think of religion as something voluntary, something we opt into or, perhaps, choose to stick with if we have been raised in a particular faith. Ahmed cannot opt out of religion at the airport. More to the point, the airport and its power structures will assume Ahmed is Muslim and therefore a threat, no matter what he does or does not believe. And that tells us something really important about religion, racialization, and our assumed freedoms—legally granted or otherwise.

You probably remember us talking about voluntarism way, way back in chapter 1, when we talked about the ability to opt out of Red Sox fandom but maybe not a racialized religion like Judaism. *Choice* is baked into the notion of religious voluntarism, and, more broadly, into ideas that govern how we are trained to think about religion.

That individual *choice* is irrelevant when we are talking about *power*.

If our comedic example, Ahmed Ahmed, can't opt *out* of religion because his face or his name read as Muslim, we can see that religion is *more than belief*. Religion coded as essentially not-white and not-Christian reads as an inherent threat to the state and world.

Lots of folks might call these experiences of religio-racism at the airport microaggressions—we feel that minimizes the trauma and violence of repeatedly being taught that *you* are a *problem*—but all these paper cuts of religio-racializations add up. All of the ways that Ahmed has no agency when it comes to self-identification? That's painful. Not because it is painful to be Middle Eastern, Arab, or Muslim (or all three), but because outsiders defining who you are and what that means, with the state's power and ability to literally criminalize you for it, is absolutely oppressive.

Let's leave Ahmed alone for a second. All he did was entertain Ilyse from 2005-ish onward when she saw the Axis of Evil tour, and now this poor man is stuck in our book.

"See something, say something" really stresses the *visual* witnessing and then witness reporting. But *hearing* something is also part of the racialized religion soup served cold at the airport. Because the languages you use can constitute a threat, a security risk, a thing to have (over)heard and reported.

After 9/11, Arabic speakers, folks who read in Arabic or languages that use Arabic scripts, and occasionally anyone who sounded sort of "foreign" became threats (foreign to whom is a great question to ask). Many Muslims, Arabs, South Asians, Northern Africans, and Southeast Asians, as well as students of those communities, histories, and languages, report surveillance when using Arabic or Arabic-looking languages.* We'll come to this in a second. But we also have a number of lawsuits and examples of Muslims being removed from flights, harassed, or otherwise surveilled in airports and on airplanes just for reading or speaking Arabic.

In 2016, as *The Independent* reported, Muslim American student "Khairuldeen Makhzoomi was 'publicly humiliated,' searched and interrogated for hours after being removed from the flight before take-off at Los Angeles International Airport." Makhzoomi spoke to his uncle on the phone in Arabic and at some point used the word

---

*Many languages use Arabic script that are not Arabic, much like many languages use the Roman alphabet but are not themselves, um, Roman. As for contemporarily spoken languages, these include the languages and multiple dialects of Arabic, Persian, Urdu, Pashto, and Kurdish.

"inshallah," an Arabic-language word that shows up in most Muslim conversations (regardless of whether they speak Arabic) because it means "God willing." This "inshallah" showed up in the court proceedings a lot. Let's unpack it for a second, just to show how troubling this scenario was.

Colloquially, Muslims say "inshallah" in many contexts, usually to express hopefulness that something will happen, a sense of humility that we mere humans cannot predict the future, and even that religious space of not wanting to "jinx" or invite the evil eye by being certain something will happen. Inshallah, in some Muslim-majority spaces and in Arabic-speaking countries, is a phrase that Muslims *and* non-Muslims use—just like many English speakers in the US say "God bless you" or "Bless you" when someone sneezes even if they are themselves not Christian or even religious. In short, inshallah is absolutely part of a religious vernacular—it invokes God, maybe even serves as a kind of prayerful, hopeful phrase—but it is also innocuous, ubiquitous, and so commonplace that many people use it without thinking twice.

Still, Makhzoomi was questioned for hours, "invasively searched," and prodded about knowing "about the martyrs" (indicating his participation in or knowledge about Islamic terrorist murders) for speaking Arabic and saying "inshallah" where someone else could hear him on an airplane. (The president of the United States can say "inshallah," as he famously did in a debate with another, oranger presidential candidate, and still expect to make his flight on time. Brown folks with names that are coded as red flags for religio-racists, not so much.) And Makhzoomi's experience is not singular.

In February 2020, just before the world shut down for COVID, Sudanese Americans Abobakkr Dirar and Mohamed Elamin tried to fly from Seattle to San Francisco. Having found their seats, Dirar texted a friend in Arabic ahead of the doors closing and final boarding calls. Another passenger, who could neither read nor speak Arabic but was nonetheless creeping on Dirar's phone, saw this text message and immediately said something about it to the Alaskan Airlines crew. Dirar and Elamin were immediately removed from the flight, subjected to extra rounds of security and questioning, and ultimately rebooked on another flight, which they were not allowed to board together—presumably *still* due to the suspicion that they were working in tandem on something Islamic-ly sinister.

CBS reported: "After airport police took Dirar's phone, authorities realized the text messages he had been sending were harmless, the lawsuit reads." This random passenger who could neither read nor write Arabic—but noticed squiggly letters—had the *power* and *authority* to set off a chain of events that caused two men significant hassle and, per their lawsuit, quite a lot of social, emotional, and mental pain.

The assumption—the cheek, the nerve, the gall, the audacity, and the gumption—that Arabic = Muslim = danger is one of racialized religion, as we're sure you can tell by now. This assumption is also one that tells us a lot about how little one has to know, how little one has to see, how little one has to hear to be able to say something *and* have something *done* within a religio-racist system. Imagine, *imagine* knowing so little and having so much power over strangers.

As if skin tone, beards, hijabs, and language weren't enough ways we see religion in the airport on the bodies of individuals and communities, there's also passports and assuming whole regions, whole nations are inherently threatening.

We have come to accept that every single person in the world needs paperwork to move about it. As we said in chapter 2, borders are lies we tell with maps and defend with bombs, but the lies that are borders still do very real harm. One simply cannot fly without identification. Flying between nation-states? You better have federal-level identification. And in a global system where some countries have more power than others, you had better believe that another layer of privilege is about passports.

Passport privilege is the idea that certain passports allow for more freedom to move about the world. And that is not just a theory: in some places, there are literal paid and documented opportunities for passports that carry privilege, like the "golden visa" or immigrant investment programs that allow wealthy people to achieve citizenship, residency, and passports (among other benefits) quickly. There are also rules about visas and entrance fees and vaccination records based upon country of origin; American passports, for example, entitle their holders to enter some 180 countries without a visa. That number is significantly less for, say, Iran.

Passport privilege has so much to do with religion, legally. In 2017, the forty-fifth president of the United States issued two executive orders known as the "Muslim ban" and the "travel ban," which were then revoked in 2021 under the leadership of the forty-sixth president of the United States. We talked about *Trump v. Hawaii* briefly in chapter 4; this US Supreme Court decision effectively says that concerns about national security outweigh the "no religious tests" provision in the US Constitution. The gist of this messy, embarrassing page of American history is actually really simple: Muslim-majority nations were targeted for being countries full of Muslims by a racist, twice-impeached leader of the USA. That later editions of the rule sidestepped the hate crime of it all by adding two non-Muslim-majority nations to the list does not undo the work of its intent; these were orders specifically targeting a religion that is linked to terror, suspicion, and anti-Americanness.

More than Trump being more foul than the gum and dog park remnants on a shoe, borders and country of origin also matter in supposedly humanitarian parts of law. We saw a global response to Ukrainian refugees as Russia tries its hand, once again, at remaking its borders with bombs. And to that we say: good. People fleeing harm should find it easy to move their bodies out of harm's way, regardless of the paperwork.

The US government has been far less forthcoming, fast, or willing to welcome Afghan asylum seekers, even though we know Afghan asylum seekers face a massive, spiraling, and potentially fatal backlog in processing their paperwork. Some news outlets report that the "US may break its promise to Afghan allies" because the US often does not actually allow these allies to seek asylum and resettle in the US. Similarly, there is both a lack of public outcry and a lack of governmental alacrity around asylum seekers from Libya, Syria, Palestine, and Yemen, who—like Ukrainians—are in the midst of brutal and ongoing war. (In fact, we've even seen measures to *bar* asylum seekers from those regions.) Data suggests similar affinities in other European nations (both in and out of the EU). Who we see as worthy of aid, who we see as worthy to become citizens, who we see as worthy of saving—a key node of asylum laws worldwide—is tied up with race, religion, and region.

SUPER DIAMOND ULTRA ELITE BOARDING FOR AMERICANS ONLY: THE US, GLOBAL POLICY, AND EXPORTING RELIGIO-RACISMS

Twenty-three years after the fact, we can say nothing more than "9/11" and have you hear a cluster of racialized religious premises and hostilities.

"Terrorist" immediately invokes religio-racist assumptions about the people who "normally" or "naturally" do terrorism and what Americans need to do to protect the world from them, the terrorists. When we look at surveys about who Americans *think of* when they think about terrorists, they *describe* people that "sound" or "look" Muslim (and, confusingly, as we have seen, may not be Muslim at all). Terrorists can be of any race, ethnicity, or religion, but when we *hear* "terrorism," globally we tend to *think* "Muslim." And we think this in cases where it doesn't really line up with the facts or data; as many, like Charles Kurzman in *The Missing Martyrs*, have proven, in the US terrorists and extremists are more likely to be white Christian nationalists than any variety of Muslim, but that doesn't mean much in the courts (of public opinion or the actual, literal judicial system).

"9/11 changed everything" sounds like a classic American over-statement, in which we think our stuff should matter to the whole world. But, in this case, it's not an overstatement: it's fact. It should feel shocking that everyone in the whole world who uses airports—whether travelers themselves or folks using items that have traveled by air—agreed to and more or less practices security in the same (American) way and has done so for over two decades, all whilst citing the same (American) incident. Rarely do changes happen all at once, and certainly rarer still as part of extant organizations (similar to the ones that govern airplanes and airspaces), and truly almost never with total and near-immediate compliance around the whole, gigantic world.

It is, in other words, kinda weird, kinda historically unique, kinda a really big deal that 9/11 changed everything for the whole world and not just the United States. It is also kinda weird, kinda historically unique, and kinda really a big deal that all this security relies on anx-ieties about racialized religion.

Everything we've said so far in this chapter takes for granted that 9/11 was big enough to make all this change happen. And while it remains the deadliest global terrorist attack to date—an ignoble title that we hope remains the case—but *size* or *scope* is not usually enough to change everything so quickly.

At the height of the COVID-19 crisis, America alone lost a 9/11's worth of people every day, for months if not years at a time. It is not the size or scope of the loss of human life that motivated these imme-diate, drastic changes in global security policies. The difference lies in the details: 9/11 gave us a palatable enemy to target, one the US seems to have permanently identified as not-white and not-Christian. The *whole world* now sees brown people with head coverings and *says* "terrorist" based on a single terrorist attack aimed exclusively at the United States.

The whole world includes nonwhite and non-Christian people and countries. Even Muslim-majority nations participate in Islamophobic global security by performing "good" Islam, respectable global citizenship, and seriousness about terrorism. 9/11 *did* change everything for everyone, because America's response to 9/11 made the whole world treat anyone who "looks Muslim" as a religious, racial threat—especially when crossing borders. Global diplomacy requires all countries—including Muslim-majority ones—to perform compliance with these religio-racist and Islamophobic policies.

Since we are claiming that the response to 9/11 is historically unique, it is important to note that it was by no means the first plane-based act of terrorism or hijacking. Nor is 9/11 the first or last time a "Western" nation was targeted, even if it is the event that created mass anxiety about flying, sky-based terrorism, and travel writ large. Airline terrorism existed as a global problem since the late 1960s; plane hijackings are nearly as old as flying itself, with the first one recorded in 1919, just sixteen years after the Wright brothers flew the world's first airplane. In the 1960s and 1970s, terrorist hijackings became more common and visible, given global media coverage. But even these high-profile hijackings, including those that originated on US soil, were not expressly affiliated with Islam or Muslims. A quick survey of those events show hijackings supported movements in Cuba, Argentina, Palestine, North Korea, Japan, Kashmir, the Philippines, and many others. In this period, there were also aircraft hijacked for reasons that were not readily determined or reported, or not deemed expressly political after all. All of which is to illustrate that while 9/11 becomes *the* moment for hijacked planes and cements an understanding of the Arab/Middle Eastern/Muslim terrorist, from the 1960s to the 1990s, airline hijacking was not expressly limited to one nationality, ethnicity, religion, region, or political movement.

Racializing Muslims as terrorists was not a new concept in 2001, even if that's when it went global. That racialization? That idea that all Muslims are suspects? That #FlyingWhileBrown is "asking for it," where "it" is harassment, detainment, delays, heightened security, "random" searches? That all went global because 9/11 happened to *Americans*. Just like we saw in the last chapter, the United States' economic and militaristic might—and its unparalleled financial domination in global aid—authorizes American priorities well beyond its borders.

Israel, for example, had incredibly stringent airline security after its experiences with hijackings in the 1960s–1970s; El Al, Israel's airline, is well known for its heightened security, which includes arming its passenger planes with missiles. But neither El Al's repeated targeting in the height of airline hijackings nor its at-the-time very strict and very unusual security rules changed airlines, airports, or air travel beyond its own practices and borders.

9/11, however, changed everything globally for everybody forever—which has everything to do with who was attacked, who did the attacking, and whose lives we see as grievable. Americans, not just any victims of hijackings or bombings, set the global tone for how we proceed with security, how we properly document travel, and who can move more freely than others. 9/11 solidified extant stereotypes about Muslim threat and codified it into policy: anti-Muslim hostility is the subtext, the base beat of "See Something, Say Something," and it affects *anyone* perceived to be Muslim.

The panic after 9/11 may have been understandable—we are old enough to remember the confusion, the terror of having collectively experienced terrorism—but the ongoing authorization and legal, social, global codification of Muslims-as-threats is religio-racialization at its finest (or worst).

That shift has *everything* to do with all the stuff we've seen in the book so far—the world religions paradigm, imperialism, race, sexuality, nationalism—even if it is also about a response to a particular and particularly horrific terrorist attack.

After 9/11, the US exported its standards for security, its definitions of the religion of terrorists, and its aid for nations that helped eradicate terrorist threats. 9/11 still dictates how we think about religion—and it still undergirds how we experience religion in airports, and how everyone is able to move around the world (or not).

COMING IN FOR A LANDING

At the start of this chapter, Ilyse and Megan shared how religion wasn't done with them at the airport. You learned too much about Ilyse's expressed breast milk and heard enough about Megan's confusion at thinking a fellow white woman was an ally only to learn she was the problem. It's not just us, though. "Assumed religious belonging at the airport as an experience of violence" is an example that is horrifically and horribly common. To start our wrap-up, we're going to share some experiences of our dearest and nearest, with names changed or omitted where we've been asked to ensure privacy.

In 2019, scholar, author, and religious literacy activist Simran Jeet Singh spoke on Twitter about how his experience as a bearded, turbaned Sikh man in the airport fundamentally changed when his daughters were old enough to ask questions. He had been pulled off the security line while his daughter watched. The TSA agent patted down his turban and swabbed his hands for explosive residue. He tells about the inquisitive look in her eyes, then writes: "What went through my daughter's mind as she watched the officer racially profile me? How long until she feels embarrassed of me, ashamed that her father wears a turban?" Singh watched as the TSA—not for the last time—taught his daughter that he is a threat.

Ilyse once waited for three hours for a Muslim friend to emerge from customs, having returned to the US from a lengthy trip abroad, in a country we might identify as Middle Eastern. She knew his flight had landed; he had texted. He was detained, his phone and computer taken away, and he was asked questions about who he was, why he went abroad, what business he had in that country, whom he met with—and then one of the guards answered his own question, indicating that they already knew the answers to what they were asking. They'd done their homework. Which makes this detention a not-so-random profiling of a very well-known and outspoken Muslim intellectual. The TSA reminded this famous scholar that they had the power to question, detain, and intimidate him because of how he looks, what his name is, and who they think he must be.

Megan once stood at an airport with a mutual friend of ours, and, as Megan is wont to do, was loudly talking about all manner of who-can-remember-what. Our friend quietly intervened and said: "Megan, you know, you use a lot of explosive, violent language when you talk—I could never do that, not here." She is a Muslim woman. The threat of surveillance and detention was enough to make our friend remind Megan that not all Americans have the same freedom of speech, especially at the airport.

We could tell a million more stories like this. Like when Ilyse's mentor won an award for his scholarship in Iran and told all his students to "expect delays at the airport from here on out" because of their names being linked. Or the ways allowing for "harassment time" is just part of how Muslims, Sikhs, and folks affected by Islamophobia—like scholars of Islam, for example—get ready to fly. The airport is, without question, an exquisite place to think about race, racialization, and who has the freedom of movement or speech, who can opt out of religion, and whose religions are safe.

In fact, it is one of the clearest ways we can tell you that religion is not done with us, because whether you are Muslim, whether you have experienced or witnessed this kind of racialized profiling and harassment, if you set foot into an airport, if you have scrambled to get your lip balm into a quart-sized bag on time, if you have bought specialized containers for your shampoo, if you have taken your shoes off, if you have allowed your body to be scanned, if you have, maybe unwittingly, scanned your surroundings for suspicious activity or second guessed that bag a mom put down for a just a second—if you've done *any* of that—you have participated in a system that is looking for specific kinds of terrorists, that values particular kinds of religions, that only understands some religious expression as "safe," "good," "apolitical." Traveling requires us to exist in, be subject to, and ultimately comply with and carry on this racist system.

You may not agree with it. You might even have protested in airports against global policies that vilify Muslims. You may abhor it. But you—*we*—have participated in a system that clearly and resolutely says: not all people can opt out of religion, here. Not all people can move freely, without suspicion, or speak a language that sounds or looks like a language associated with one religion. We have participated willingly or not in a system that makes assumptions about religion based upon appearances and assumptions about race, nationality, language, and sexuality.

And that's the real flight risk, no? That after 9/11 we, as a global community, fled to a new normal in which religion functions differently for different groups legally and tangibly in something as simple as traveling. We have so normalized, so naturalized the idea that some religions require or support violence to such a degree that we all submit to invasive protocols, assist in surveillance, engage in global policy, and leave unasked questions about whether this protects us—and whom it might harm.

The risk in all this is that we make religion a choice for some but a mandate for others; that we see some religions as permanently foreign to, say, the US or Europe; that we see some religions as inherently part of places like, say, the Middle East or Africa or Asia, and treat people from those places with suspicion. The risk is that we let religion sneak around, lurk under the floorboards, in such a way that it becomes hard to name it, hard to see it, hard to demand that this system be made more just.

▪ ▪ ▪

We cannot change what systems assume about us: institutions like the TSA use the racialized, religionized categories they inherit from the creation of the category of religion, from the world religions model, from the way we built race out of religion, from the way our systems use religion to control our bodies. But learning to see religion at work in the world—in the airport and beyond—is the first fragile step toward remaking these systems in ways that allow all of us to be different from one another, safer, and more free.

▪ ▪ ▪ ▪ ▪ ▪ ▪ ▪ ▪ ▪

FURTHER READING

Caleb Iyer Elfenbein, *Fear in Our Hearts: What Islamophobia Tells Us About America* (New York: NYU Press, 2022)

Todd H. Green, *Presumed Guilty: Why We Shouldn't Ask Muslims to Condemn Terrorism* (Minneapolis: Fortress Press, 2018)

Deepa Kumar, *Islamophobia and the Politics of Empire* (Chicago: Haymarket Books, 2012)

Arun Kundnani, *The Muslims Are Coming! Islamophobia, Extremism, and the Domestic War on Terror* (London: Verso, 2015)

Charles Kurzman, *The Missing Martyrs: Why Are There So Few Muslim Terrorists?* (New York: Oxford University Press, 2018)

Nadine Naber, "'Look, Mohammed the Terrorist Is Coming!' Cultural Racism, Nation-Based Racism, and the Intersectionality of Oppressions After 9/11," in *Race and Arab Americans Before and After 9/11: From Invisible Citizens to Visible Subjects*, ed. Amaney A. Jamal and Nadine Christine Naber (Syracuse, NY: Syracuse University Press, 2008)

Saher Selod, *Forever Suspect: Racialized Surveillance of Muslim Americans in the War on Terror* (New Brunswick, NJ: Rutgers University Press, 2018)

FURTHER LISTENING ON KEEPING IT 101

(E106) "You Might Be Done with Religion, but Religion Is Not Done with You"

(E410) "You Still Don't Know About Islam, Part 2"

(E506) "INCORRECT: Jihad"

WHAT DO YOU DO WITH THE RELIGION THAT IS NOT DONE WITH YOU?

*in which we humbly suggest you consider calendars
as a tool for becoming better neighbors*

We don't know about you, friends, but that last chapter left us feeling like we just got off a long and bumpy flight. We've covered a *lot* of ground in this book. We talked about what religion *is* (and isn't), how global histories of imperialism still shape how we think about religion (and how our maps work), how religion and race cannot be separated neatly, how religion is political, and how religion is not done with any of us. You might be feeling, dare we say, disoriented?

With all this new information at your fingertips, it might be tricky to think about where to go next. Now that you know that religion isn't done with you, what do you do with a problem like religion? To pastiche some of our favorite activist-thinkers: once we know better we do better, and while naming a problem sometimes makes us the problem, the right sort of problem can be very good trouble indeed. So let's get out there and make good trouble. Necessary trouble. Let's trouble religion! Not by ignoring it or insisting it go away, but by making more space for more people to be religious in more ways— and fighting for justice for all people, regardless of whether they're religious or not.

If you're wondering where to start, don't worry! We're going to end this book with what we in the business like to call an "applied learning exercise." Let's think of it as homework: a small thing you can do in your own life—whether that's privately, as you move through the world, or publicly, in any of your roles Out There.

Remember way back in the introduction when we asked you if you had a phone? And we said mazel tov! You just found religion in your pants, because your phone almost certainly has a calendar on it.

This wasn't just a silly joke. (It is *also* a silly joke, though.) Calendars are not just proof that religion isn't done with us—they're also a simple way for you to make seemingly small but potentially high-impact change in your community.

This is because calendars are yet another seemingly neutral informational tool—like maps!—that actually makes choices about which information to include and whose events are worth observing. Remember when we said that the world religions paradigm means some religious communities literally fall off the map? Even more religious communities fall right off your standard, preloaded calendar.

Because, sorry to say, religion is so not done with us that it shapes how we measure time itself. And we're not just talking about solstices and equinoxes for witches or the precise moment observant Muslims get to break their fasts during Ramadan. The standard Google calendar app—downloaded half a billion times, used by one in three people who use a calendar app anywhere in the world—is making significant political choices in which religious holidays to include and which to omit. This goes for every other calendar, printed or digital, ever created. Calendars show us religious history but also religious inclusion and exclusion at work in our daily lives.

In Western countries, our standard calendar is the Gregorian calendar—which, as you might remember from the introduction, is the eponymous calendar of Roman Catholicism's own Pope Gregory XIII. The year everyone agrees it is? (And by everyone we mean banks, governments, and the military—more institutions also deeply shaped by religion, but we don't have time to get into that now because this is the end of the book.) The year we agree it is, is a direct product of Christian imperialism. That year corresponds to Jesus+N, where N stands for however many years it's been since the year we used to think Jesus was born in.

(Jesus was probably born in the year of Jesus minus 5, give or take. Calendars are less math than politics, is what we're saying.)

We very sincerely hope you did not think that all people in all times and places—including our own—measured time as Jesus+N, and any time before Jesus as counting down to Jesus. Not once did Julius say: Hey, Brutus? Is it 50 years till Christ or 49? Not once did Brutus reply: it sure is weird that we experience time forward but are counting backward to some point. And, yes, the more conscientious among us might write CE (common era) rather than AD (*anno domini*, i.e., the year of The [Christian] Lord whose devotees colonized nearly all the countries in the world). But dates are still Jesus+N no matter how you suffix them.

And, sure, there are "alternative" calendars—but ask yourselves, alternative to what? Did you guess "standard Western Christian holiday observances"? We bet you did. Because obviously the folks who use those calendars don't think of them as auxiliary. Jews, Muslims, Hindus, Buddhists, Pagans, and many more religious communities have their own calendars; even those tradition-specific calendars often vary according to language and region.

Different religious communities measure time differently, too. Why does a standard day run midnight to midnight instead of, as in Jewish practice, roughly sunset to sunset? Different calendars also show us different communities' ways of marking seasons. The Jewish New Year (Rosh Hashanah) is in the fall, corresponding to harvest seasons. Persian New Year (Nowruz) is in the spring, corresponding to when the world wakes back up, and even though a majority of Persian folk are also Muslim, Nowruz *is not* Islamic New Year, which is typically observed on the first of the Islamic month of Muharram. Across Asia and in many different religions, Lunar New Year happens between the end of January and the end of February, because it is based on the lunisolar calendar.

Time is, in short, complicated—and the way we measure time is all tangled up in religion. This means that on a "standard" or "secular" calendar, *your* Jewish, Persian, Hindu, Buddhist, lunar, Islamic, etc., calendar will always be *secondary*.

Because no matter where you are, whose holidays are recognized by the state, schools, courts, and banks reflect the dominant culture. Ditto whose holidays are relegated to an interfaith calendar. Non-Western countries often have calendars that reflect Christian observances be-cause European Christian imperialism shapes how we measure time all over the world. This is because Christian imperialism created the West's calendar, which means any country that wants to do business with a Western country has to accommodate the West's calendar. The really short version? Ramadan is definitely on calendars created in Muslim-majority countries, but Christmas is on calendars all over the world, no matter what religion (or lack thereof, in China's case) dominates your country.

But this epilogue isn't (just) about bumming you out and remind-ing you that religion will always have its chocolate up in your peanut butter. It's about showing you how and where you can use religion to make change for a more just world. It's as easy as 1-2-3.

Step 1: Look at your calendar. Which holidays does your standard cal-endar app include? (We will bet you five dollars that no matter where you're reading this book, Christmas is on your calendar.) Which hol-idays are missing? You might not even know! And that's okay. We can give you a few to search for. Does your calendar mention Ramadan? Yom Kippur? Diwali? Are there other important religious observances missing? Make some quick notes about what you find.

Step 2: Look at some other calendars. Now that you've looked at the calendar on your phone, check the one for your workplace or your school or your local library. Same questions as above: Who's included? Who's missing? Which is to say: Who's marked as important? Worth thinking about? Actually existing in your community?

As above, we encourage you to start by checking whether your school/job/etc. calendar includes significant religious holidays and seasons like Ashura or Rosh Hashana or Vaisakhi. Make some quick notes about any significant oversights or omissions.

Step 3: Be the problem who makes good trouble. Here's the important but also honestly pretty easy part. Pick one (1) calendar from your community that leaves off an important season or holiday from a religious tradition other than your own. Write a nice email or leave a polite message requesting that the community you're a part of do this one small thing to make space for different ways of being religious.

That's it.

No, seriously.

That's the entire assignment.

This might seem like a really small thing to do—honestly, maybe even too small? But there's no amount of trying to make our communities more inclusive of marginalized folks that's too small to matter. That the assignment is so small is the best part about it. You can do it today! Right now! Will your email or phone call change the whole world? Of course not. But it might be a first step toward making your Jewish, Muslim, Hindu, and otherwise othered neighbors feel more at home in your shared community.

For Ilyse? This looks like the constant reminding of schools that non-Christians are people and maybe we could put the holidays kids and families might take off, be in houses of worship, or just may not want "extras" for on the district-wide calendars. She does not like the interfaith app option, nor the "see also" bits. She wants to stop the awkwardness of reminding the PTO president for the third year in a row to not book school picture day on Yom Kippur. Or international night during Ramadan. Or a school play on Lunar New Year. For Megan? Megan once emailed an interfaith chaplain before the beginning of her first semester on the job to ask about the inclusion of Bahá'í holidays and the omission of solstices and equinoxes. And when she was told that "we can't include everybody," she sent some more emails. This is also how she wound up singing "We All Come from the Goddess" at a multifaith event, but that is another story that shall be told another time. And lest you think we killjoys always get this stuff right, you should also know that Megan has on at least one occasion attempted to schedule a meeting with Ilyse on Yom Kippur. (Because Yom Kippur was on her calendar, but the dumb calendar started Yom Kippur at midnight, not sunset the day before.) But when that happened, Megan apologized and rescheduled—because when you know better, you do better. Right? Of course right.

Chances are if you belong to a minoritized religious community, you're already doing this work. We are too! Ilyse emails her kiddos' principal and pops into Board of Ed meetings. Megan avoids scheduling exams when students are likely to be fasting and triple-checks her calendars, plural, before scheduling meetings with Ilyse in September. This work matters because when we fall off calendars, we fall out of communities. That makes all of us less safe and less free.

But here's the thing about justice, friends—vulnerable folks shouldn't have to do all the work! No one should have to make the choice between resigning themselves and their families to irrelevance and invisibility or using their one wild and precious life to call the PTO president *again* because picture day is on Yom Kippur *again*. What if we all looked out for one another, not because we feel obligated, but because that's how we get free?

You don't have to take on the whole world, or even your whole state! You can just ask your local school board to consider how the calendar affects religious students: days off for religious observance (and the ways teachers can move tests and major assignments off holidays); mindfulness about religious students' fasting schedules during holiday seasons; cafeteria options that reflect religious observance (fish on Fridays, perhaps; availability of dining halls after sunset); just *mentioning* non-Christian holidays over the loudspeakers. Does your school put up Santas and Christmas trees as "seasonal and secular" decorations? Do you really think that's just seasonal or secular? (As non-Christians, let us let you know: not so much.) And if not, how could we mark the season in a more inclusive way?

You can bring up calendars at work. You can be the person who—instead of asking your Hindu coworker when Diwali is—finds out when Diwali is and tries not to schedule after-hours events that day so your coworker can go and celebrate how they want. It really can be as simple as that.

And if you're an overachiever like Ilyse, you can take it a step further. That might look like asking for policy shifts: if your company *closes* for Christmas, Christians and former Christians and secular Christians all get (paid?) days off. But the Jews, Muslims, Hindus, Zoroastrians, Jains, Sikhs, Buddhists, Bahá'í, who might not care if they have those days off—but might *definitely* want (paid?) holiday observation days *at different times in the year?* What if your place of work had that policy: What if everyone got religious observance days off, instead of just Christians? Because guess what: minoritized religious people use personal days for religious observances, often outing themselves to do so, which for some folks is an awkward or even risky move. (Megan had to do this at Northeastern, and even working in liberal Massachusetts is not a guarantee your employer will be cool with you calling out of work as witchy). Christians do not have to do that; their major day is always already off in most professions—and if it isn't, usually comes with bonus pay in many places in the US and Europe.

Advocating for policy changes often draws an atheist or two out of the woodwork claiming that eliminating *all* religious observances is the fairest outcome for everyone. Don't be that dude. (And, sorry, it's usually a dude. A white dude. Although sometimes it's Neil deGrasse Tyson, for reasons that escape us.) Atheists should get days off too! Y'all want to observe Isaac Asimov's birthday? G'head. More flexibility and more rest are good for everybody.

What else can you do with calendars?

You tell us!

Now you know that calendars are political—which means you can start agitating for our calendars to have better politics. Go be a problem who makes good trouble for great justice.

That's your homework.

Class dismissed.

ACKNOWLEDGMENTS

This is a work of serious scholarship, silly jokes, and pure joy (killed and otherwise). We are so baffled, so delighted, and so grateful to have pulled off what feels like The Great Nerd Caper: a project that let an expert in American minority religions and an expert in South Asian Islam collaborate on something neither of them could or would have written alone. But sometimes when two people fall crazy stupid intellectually in love with one another, they just can't help but make a book about it. (Ask your parents how it happens.)

This collaboration—beyond our years of building a chosen family together—started as a podcast. We couldn't have done that work without support; we wouldn't have done this work if that work never happened. We are so fortunate to have had our public scholarship supported by the New England Humanities Consortium's Seed Grant (2020), the University of Vermont (UVM) Humanities Center Public Humanities Fellowship (2021), UVM's Research Enhancement in the Arts, Creative Disciplines, and Humanities Grant (2022–23), and the Luce Foundation & American Academy of Religion Advancing Public Scholarship Grant (2022). We are grateful for the support and recognition of the Amplify Podcast Network as well as the Religion Communicators Council for their Wilbur Award of Merit (2023). We are also eternally grateful to the folks who have listened and keep listening to us yell and scream and laugh and swear on *Keeping It 101*.

We are additionally indebted to the University of Vermont's Religion Department and Peter J. Seybolt Faculty Fund in Asian Studies for making the historic maps in chapter 2 printable, as well as illustrator Chrissy Kurpeski for (re)making the maps in a way that's legible in this century and format.

Ilyse spent her time at the University of Birmingham as a 2022–23 US Fulbright Scholar writing this book while researching the next. She is very appreciative of Andrew Davies and Charlotte Hempel's warm welcomes and collegiality while navigating the UK, being away from her family, and managing an overzealous research agenda. (Relatedly, we are extremely grateful for the Scotch whiskey we indulged in after finishing this book in Edinburgh, and for all the Scots who did not visibly mind the post-submission, mid-street, post-whiskey dancing to the Beastie Boys that followed. May we not see no cars forever.)

As Mary Hunt teaches us, it is only together that we are a genius. We've made it a motto of sorts—because we think killing joy is a team sport, an ensemble performance—and so, of course, we have many collaborators to thank, in writing, profusely and for posterity.

A who's who of folks who have consistently helped move this project forward, helped us think more clearly, helped us hone our tone, and helped us see the bigger picture include: Andrew Aghapour, Tom Borchert, Katherine Brennan, Vicki Brennan, Alex Castellano, Juliana Finch, Shreena Gandhi, Jonas Hart, Melvin James Kaminsky, Hannah McGregor, Kristian Petersen, Jorge Rodríguez, omid safi, Simran Jeet Singh, Luis Vivanco, Judith Weisenfeld, Evie Wolfe, and Rachel Zieff.

We are buoyed by the support, friendship, love, and stern "get this done" looks of Emmie Aghapour, Kelly J. Baker, Joy Carter, Jen Conetta, Matthew Corwin, Kathleen M. Foody, Jay Garvey, Deena Blair Goodman, Tommy McCann, Meghan Tiernan-Fisher, Lydia Willsky-Ciollo, and Dark Web Rosh Hodesh for being the inspiration to speak and write in a way any curious person could understand.

Special in-writing love must be afforded to Kevin, Sela, and Simon Morgenstein Fuerst, Megan's favorite brother-in-law, niece, and nephew—and the best team Ilyse has ever had the joy to both make and play for.

Megan would also like to formally thank Adderall for making this and, indeed, any and all writing possible.

We also owe our sincerest thanks to the family and friends who tune in despite/because of our swearing; the students around the world who are listening (and the professors who are telling them to); Ilyse's students in REL2050 and REL1050 who read draft manuscripts; the erstwhile Twitter community we learned so much from; our therapists; our massage therapists; Ilyse's physical therapists; our primary motivators, spite and justice; and Love Island UK, because we are semi-messy bitches who live for drama (and Chris and Kem).

This book would just be a Google doc if not for Amy Caldwell, Nicole-Anne Keyton, Marcy Barnes, Susan Lumenello, and everyone else at Beacon who worked to make this book a real boy on our behalf.

People are, as we will not stop saying, a big, wonderful, terrible, overwhelming, exhausting, irreplaceable mess, doing all manner of big, wonderful, terrible, overwhelming, exhausting, irreplaceably messy things. We're so grateful you're willing to mess around with us, dear reader, learning and thinking with us—and, dare we hope—taking this information and doing something with it to make our world a more just, more livable place.

INDEX

abortion, 112–15; American support for, 98; and birth control, 16; "heartbeat" laws, 113; Jewish law and, 113; Mexico City Policy ("global gag rule"), 114–16; as nonreligious issue, 111; regulation in Muslim-majority countries, 113; removal of constitutional protections, 99, 109; right to, 110; and US foreign policy, 114–16. *See also Dobbs v. Jackson Women's Health Organization*; pregnancy; *Roe v. Wade*

African Traditional religions, 88

Ahmed, Ahmed, 129–32

aid, international 38, 114, 116, 137

airports, 120; Islamophobia in, 132, 135, 142; religion in, 121, 131–32. *See also* September 11th terrorist attacks

Alexander VI (pope), 44

American Empire: and forced conversion, 90; in Hawaii, 92; preference for Protestantism, 29; and race, 68; relationship to European Christian imperialism, 77; resistance to, 89; and science, 79; use of racialized religion, 87, 91; use of religion, 92

American Legion v. American Humanist Association, 108

antisemitism, 12, 29; and European Christian imperialism, 45; hate crimes, 13, 32; in the United States, 74

Arabic, 10, 133–35. *See also* language

Asian Exclusion Act, 103

asylum, 22, 37, 136–37

atheism, 31, 100; views on abortion, 16

Axis of Evil Comedy Tour, 129–30

Bahá'í, 150; religious observance days, 151

Baldwin, James; defining religion, 7; on relationship between race and religion, 86; on systems, 39, 98; on whiteness, 80

Bangladesh: Islam in, 60

baseball, 19–33

Battle of Wounded Knee, 89

beards, 129, 141; profiling based on, 135

belief, 30; constitutional protection of, 106; "god gene," 21; importance of, 39, 121; lack of, 31; vs. practice, 107–8; and religious voluntarism, 29; theism, 30

Biden, Joseph R., 136; use of "inshallah," 134

bin Laden, Osama, 130

bodies, 72; autonomy of, 99, 104–6, 109, 111–13; and identity, 72; imperial control of, 72; national, 38; racial, 69, 72; regulation of, 98, 106, 109, 116; religious, 26, 32, 92; and socially constructed hierarchies, 71; value of, 21, 98

borders, 54, 135; concept of, 41; in Kashmir, 63; made by religion, 37–38, 46, 56, 61–63; in Palestine, 64. *See also* maps

British Empire: in Burma, 57; and forced conversion, 43; in India, 54–63; in North America, 76; and the Partition of India, 60; preference for Protestantism, 28; resistance to, 89; in South Asia, 54–63

British Transport Police: and terrorism, 127

Buck v. Bell, 103

Buddhism: calendar of, 147–48; in Burma, 62; lack of deities, 30 as "major religion," 36, 48; religious observance days, 151; in South Asia, 57, 62; in Sri Lanka, 62

Burma: British Empire in, 57; Buddhism in, 62

Burwell v. Hobby Lobby Stores, 16, 92, 131

Bush, George W., 129

calendars, 147–52; and Christian imperialism, 148; Christian as standard, 17, 37, 146–48; Gregorian, 41, 146; and religious seasons, 149; in school, 150; "secular," 148. *See also* religious observance days; time

Catholicism: Lent, 151; views on abortion, 15, 111–12. *See also* Roman Catholic Church

Cherokee Nation, 77

Chinese Exlusion Act, 103

Christian nationalism, 4, 94, 100, 120; and abortion, 99; and calendars, 100; and currency, 100; fears of white decline, 103, 108; and foreign policy, 114; and imperialism, 114–15; Ku Klux Klan, 73; and Mormonism, 108; Proud Boys, 73; Qanon "Shaman," 92; and religious extremism, 137; resistance to, 89; and schools, 100; and secularism, 103; sexual ethics of, 99, 108–10, 113–15; and terrorism, 137; and US legal system, 93, 100–104, 108, 116; and US political system, 98; and the US Supreme Court, 73, 88–89, 104–16; and voting, 100; and white supremacy, 99, 108, 115; and white women's rights, 81–87. *See also* American Empire; Supreme Court, US

Christianity: as American, 108; Anglicanism, 28, 50; as cultural norm, 12; European, 38–53, 64, 66, 68, 72–80, 94, 101–3, 148; forced conversion to, 43, 49, 90; in India, 60; justifications for slavery, 78; as "major religion," 36; in North Africa, 51–52; relationship to Islam, 50; and sexuality, 99, 102, 107–15; tacit establishment of, 32; and white supremacy, 12, 43, 51, 60, 67, 73, 82, 86, 99, 103, 108, 128. *See also* Christian nationalism; *names of specific denominations*

Citizens United v. Federal Election Commission, 16

colonialism, 45, 46; in Africa, 51–52; American Christian, 78; in the Americas, 66, 76–77; and calendars, 17; in Canada, 77; the "civilizing mission," 50; definition of, 43; European

Christian, 78; forced conversion, 43, 49, 90; land theft, 72, 77; in Mexico, 77; relationship to imperialism, 76; theories of, 61. *See also* imperialism; *names of specific empires*
Confucianism: and misdesignation as a religion, 30
contraception, 112–13, 115; access to, 16; right to, 110
Coptic Christianity, 51–52
COVID-19, 134, 138

Dakota Access Pipeline, 89, 92–93
Daoism: lack of deities, 30
Declaration of Independence, 73
Department of Homeland Security, 126–27
Dirar, Abobakkr, 134–35
Dobbs v. Jackson Women's Health Organization, 99, 102, 109, 112; and Christian nationalism, 114; and personhood, 113; as violation of the First Amendment, 113. *See also* abortion; *Roe v. Wade*
Doctrine of Discovery, 44, 48, 75, 91–92; application by non-Catholic powers, 77
Doctrine of Terra Nullius, 78

Eisenstadt v. Baird, 110
Elamin, Mohamed, 134–35
Employment Division v. Smith, 91, 114
eugenics, 108, 109–10; forced sterilization, 103

Fanon, Frantz, 61, 77
feminism, 4, 5; and white Christianity, 86; and white supremacy, 81–87
First Amendment, 37, 90, 105, 131; and Christian nationalism, 116;

establishment clause of, 105–6, 113, 116; freedom of speech, 142; free exercise clause of, 105–7, 116. *See also* US Constitition; *names of specific cases*
food: kosher, 8; Lent, 151; religious food practices, 8–10, 37, 93, 151
Francis (pope), 92
freedom of speech, 142. *See also* First Amendment
free movement: restrictions on, 143
French Empire: and forced conversion, 43; in North America, 76; resistance to, 89
Freud, Sigmund, 72

Ghost Dance, 89. *See also* Indigenous American religion
Gregory XIII (pope), 41, 147
Griswold v. CT, 110, 112–13

head coverings, 129, 138; Bill 21, 32; hijab, 25, 32, 128, 135; profiling based on, 135; turbans, 25, 29, 32, 128–29, 141. *See also* Islamophobia; Sikhi
healthcare, 15, 16; abortion as, 98; sexual and reproductive, 98–99, 115. *See also* abortion; contraception; pregnancy
hijab. *See* head coverings
Hinduism: British view of, 62; calendar of, 147–48; caste system, 14; different practices of, 48; in India, 55, 60; polytheism, 40, 88; religious observance days, 149, 151; ritual, 14; in South Asia, 55, 60; and yoga, 14
HIV/AIDS, 115
homosexuality: discrimination against, 91; in India, 108; and marriage, 110, 112–13; regulation of, 89, 102

identity: and intersectionality, 71, 130; as social construct, 69, 71–72

Ifá, 88

immigration: US restrictions on, 103, 135

imperialism, 45; American Christian, 68, 77, 79, 87, 90; and calendars, 147–48; civil service, 49; vs. colonialism, 43; and data, 49, 54–55, 61; definition of, 43; European Christian, 39–43, 68, 72, 77, 79, 94, 101–3; Muslim, 42; and "primitive" vs. "civilized" religion, 88; use of religion, 29, 36–38, 54–63, 92; white Christian, 99. *See also names of specific empires*

India, 63; borders of, 63; British Empire in, 54–63; Christianity in, 60; Hinduism in, 54–63; Islam in, 52, 54–63; legal codes, 102–3; Partition of, 54–63

Indigenous American religion, 87, 91, 95; American Indian Religious Freedom Act, 89; appropriation of, 92–93; minoritized, 90; and peyote, 89, 91; relationship to race, 68. *See also Indigenous Americans*

Indigenous Americans: American Indian Movement, 89; forced conversion of, 90; genocide of, 89; and land, 13; myth of the "Vanishing Indian," 87; residential school system, 90–91; strategies of colonial resistance, 89, 92

Inter Caetera, 44

international law, 38

intersectionality, 71, 130

Islam, 11, 50; in Bangladesh, 60; calendar of, 147–48; and concept of religion, 40; dress practices, 25, 32, 101, 128, 135; as "Eastern" religion, 50, 53;

in Europe, 52; and European Christian imperialism, 51; as global religion, 52; in India, 52, 55, 60; in the Middle East, 52; in North Africa, 52; in Pakistan, 60; racialization of, 121, 128–29, 132, 139; relationship to Christianity, 50; religious observance days, 151; in South Asia, 55, 60; in Spain, 52; and terrorism, 125, 137; as threat to European dominance, 48; as unique threat after September 11th attacks, 137–40; use of "inshallah," 134; views on abortion, 16; women, 32. *See also Islamophobia*

Islamophobia, 11–13, 130; in airports, 123, 134–35, 142; and European Christian imperialism, 45; after September 11th attacks, 128–132, 140; and Sikhs, 29, 128–29, 141; in US law, 139

Israel: boundaries of, 64; response to plane hijackings, 140

Jainism: lack of deities, 30; religious observance days, 151

Jammu, 62–63

January 6th Insurrection, 92

Japanese internment, 72

Jerusalem: and European colonialism, 53

Judaism: calendar of, 147–48; dietary law, 8–10; dress practices of, 32; as "major" religion, 36, 48; monotheistic, 88; practices of, 30; religious observance days, 151; views on abortion, 16

Kashmir, 62, 139

language, 135; and Islam, 10; profiling based on, 133–35. *See also Arabic*

Lawrence v. Texas, 110, 112–13
legal precedence, 112; operation
 of, 102
*Little Sisters of the Poor Saints Peter
 and Paul Home v. Pennsylvania*, 16
Loving v. Virginia, 110, 112–13
Luther, Martin, 41

Makhzoomi, Khairuldeen, 133–34
maps, 54–64; Partition of India,
 54–63
marriage: interracial marriage, 103,
 110; polygamous marriage, 103,
 107; right to, 110, 112–13
*Masterpiece Cakeshop v. Colorado
 Civil Rights Commission*, 89
Mexico City policy, 115
Middle East, 53; Axis of Evil Comedy Tour, 129–30; Islam in, 52;
 in relation to "the West," 52–53;
 and science, 42
minoritized religions, 4, 38, 150–51;
 and religious protection, 74. *See
 also* First Amendment
modernity: built on Mus-
 lim science, 41–42; as
 European-created concept,
 41–42; and world religions
 paradigm, 29
monotheism, 39, 47, 88
Moral Majority, 111
Mormonism, 107, 114; Smith,
 Joseph, 108; as uncivilized, 107
"Muslim ban," 105, 136
Muslim-majority nations, 53,
 135–37; calendars of, 148; participation in Islamophobic security
 measures, 138

nation: concept of, 41; definition
 of, 101; national identity, 38;
 nationalism, 97
Nepal: Buddhism in, 62
new religious movements, 36

nones, 2, 13
nongovernmental organizations,
 37, 115
North America: European colonization of, 76–77. *See also*
 imperialism
North Korea, 129, 139

Obergefell v. Hodges, 110, 112–13
Omar, Ilhan, 101
orientalism, 45, 50, 55. *See also*
 Said, Edward

paganism, 90, 92, 100; calendar,
 147; as invocation of white
 supremacy, 92
Pakistan: borders of, 63; British
 partition of, 62; Islam in, 60
Palestine, 139; asylum seekers from,
 137; boundaries of, 64; and Jesus
 Christ, 53
papacy, 78; and imperialism, 76.
 See also Doctrine of Discovery;
 Doctrine of Terra Nullius; *Inter
 Caetera*
Partition of India, 54–63. *See also*
 maps
passports, 135–37; restrictions
 based in religion, 136
personhood: corporate, 16; fetal,
 113; of pregnable people, 113
*Peyote Way Church of God, Inc. v.
 Thornburgh*, 89
plane hijackings, 139. *See also* September 11th terrorist attacks
polygamy. *See* marriage
polytheism: African Traditional
 religions, 88; and belief, 30;
 Hinduism, 10, 40
pornography, 110
Portuguese Empire, 44, 76; and
 forced conversion, 43; in India,
 57
Pratt, Richard Henry, 89

pregnancy, 110; Islamic law and, 113; Jewish law and, 113. *See also* abortion

prejudice, 74; queerphobia, 70, 89–91, 102; state-sanctioned, 129; unconscious bias, 70. *See also* racism

privacy, right to, 109–12. See also *Roe v. Wade*; US Constitution

profiling, 123, 142; based on dress practices, 135; based on language, 133, 135, 143; based on name, 131; racial, 131, 135; religious, 29, 32, 131–32. *See also* September 11th terrorist attacks; surveillance, state

Protestantism, 17, 28–29, 41; alliance with Catholics over abortion, 111; English Reformation, 50, 76; German Reformation, 41; views on abortion, 111

Punjab: Sikhi in, 57, 62

Qanon "shaman", 92

race, 46; changing meanings over time, 72, 74; conceptual origins in America, 66; scientific arguments for racial hierarchy, 78; as social construct, 68, 72, 79. *See also* racism; whiteness; white supremacy

racialization: of ethnic identity, 130; of geographic identity, 130; of Islam, 129; of religious identity, 88–89, 121, 128–32, 139–42

racism, 129; anti-Asian, 13, 74, 103; anti-Black, 12–13, 94; anti-native, 94; as political liability, 111; and religious identity, 123–24; scientific, 78–80. *See also* prejudice; white supremacy

Reagan, Ronald, 115

religion: anticolonial resistance, 38; assumed to stand in for Christianity, 75; and civility, 11; as community, 81; creation of concept, 38; on currency, 100; defining, 8, 22, 30–31, 40–41, 46–47, 108; as descriptive category, 22; establishment of, 105; etymology of, 45; European definition of, 47; forced conversion, 43, 49, 90; as identity, 32; and power, 23; racialization of, 121, 128–29, 132, 139; and relationship to race, 68; in schools, 100; as a social construct, 21, 23, 69; social recognition of, 15, 22; as system, 6–8, 11, 33, 69; as a tool of imperialism, 36, 38, 43, 45, 60, 66, 73, 78; as a tool of liberation, 81, 87; as universal concept, 36; in the US legal system, 100; in voting, 8, 100. *See also names of specific religions*

religious extremism, 128; Muslim, 124, 137; US focus on Islamic terrorism, 124–5; which religions are designated "extreme", 143; white Christian Nationalist, 137. *See also* Christian nationalism; terrorism

religious freedom, 116; and abortion, 99; freedom of expression, 142; for Indigenous Americans, 89, 91; limits to, 107; Muslim, 129; separation of church and state, 32, 104, 105. *See also* First Amendment

Religious Freedom Restoration Act, 91. *See also* Indigenous American religion

religious observance days, 146, 151; and Christian nationalism, 99; Christmas, 17, 99, 148; as

establishment, 105; Islamic New Year, 148; Lunar New Year, 148, 150; on standard calendar, 17, 148, 149; and world religions paradigm, 37; Yom Kippur, 149–51
religious seasons, 150; Ashura, 149; Diwali, 149, 151; Lent, 151; Ramadan, 149, 150; Rosh Hashana, 147, 149; Vaisakhi, 149
religious superiority, 47–48
religious tests, 37, 105, 136. *See also* US Constitution
religious voluntarism, 20; limitations of, 28, 121, 132, 143; and racilialized religion, 132
Revolutionary War (United States), 77
Reynolds v. United States, 107–8, 114
ritual, 26, 30; yoga as, 14
Roe v. Wade, 102, 109–13
Roman Catholic Church, 48; and colonialism, 76; as colonizer, 91; control of Western Europe, 41; healthcare, 15; and residential schools, 90–91. *See also* Catholicism; colonialism; Doctrine of Discovery; imperialism; papacy; *names of specific popes*
RuPaul's Drag Race, 69

Said, Edward, 45, 55
science: concept of, 41; as construct, 66; denialism, 17; European Christian, 42; of Indigenous American peoples, 76; medieval, 42; Muslim, 42; and race, 66, 78, 79; and slavery, 78; as a tool of imperialism, 42, 79
secularism, 12, 151; and Western society, 11; and white Christian values, 104

September 11th terrorist attacks, 124, 133, 137; global aftermath, 120, 124, 137–38, 140; responses to, 125, 139. *See also* Islamophobia; War on Terror
settler colonialism, 75; and the Doctrine of Discovery, 49; and mapping, 77; in North America, 77; process of, 76, 93; and race, 79; and whiteness, 80. *See also* colonialism; imperialism
Seventh-day Adventism, 106
sex, 97, 112; nonreproductive, 103, 110, 113, 115; reproductive, 115; same-sex sexual acts, 102. *See also* abortion; pregnancy
sexuality, 97; and Christianity, 102; criminalization of homosexuality, 102; regulation of, 102–4; representative of American values, 111; as a social construct, 97. *See also* homosexuality; *Lawrence v. Texas*; *Obergefell v. Hodges*
Sherbert v. Verner, 106
Sikhi, 36; and Islamophobia, 11, 29, 32, 141–42; as minoritized religion, 48; and the Partition of India, 62; profiling of, 122, 123, 128; in Punjab, 57; religious observance days, 151; in South Asia, 56–57, 62; turbans, 25, 29, 32, 128–29, 141; and world religions model, 62. *See also* head coverings; South Asia
Singh, Simran Jeet, 141
slavery, 49; abolitionism, 81–87; Christian justifications for, 74, 78; as fundamental to US economy, 79; of indigenous Caribbean peoples, 78; as inherited condition, 78; and science, 78; as a tool of imperialism, 75; transatlantic slave trade, 52, 77, 79

Smith, J. Z., 22, 40, 87

South Asia, 54, 63; British colonization of, 76; British Empire in, 54–63; British partition of, 62; Buddhism in, 56; Christianity in, 56–57, 60; Hinduism in, 54–63; historical views of sexuality, 102; Islam in, 54–63; Sikhi in, 56

Spanish Empire, 44, 76; conquistadors, 76; and forced conversion, 43; missionaries, 76; resistance to, 89

spiritual but not religious, 2, 13, 20–21

Sri Lanka: Buddhism in, 62

Stewart, Potter, 110

Stowe, Harriet Beecher, 86

Supreme Court, US, 131, 136; and abortion, 102, 104; Alito, Samuel, 112; and corporate personhood, 16; and marriage, 107, 110, 112; and religious freedom, 73, 89, 91, 104–8, 114; religious makeup of, 112; and sexuality, 107–10, 112; Sotomayor, Sonia, 105; Thomas, Clarence, 112. *See also names of specific cases*

surveillance, state: in airports, 120, 123, 133; of Arabic speakers, 133; of Muslims, 126; after 9/11, 124; public participation in, 127, 134–35, 143; of Sikhs, 123

systems, 46, 61, 98, 116, 119, 143; carceral, 93; healthcare, 15; how do they work, 70; of oppression, 70; and power, 33; religion in, 8; religious, 33. *See also* US legal system

terrorism, 128–29, 137, 138; Ku Klux Klan, 73; Muslim, 124–25. *See also* September 11th terrorist attacks

time, 146; measured differently by religious communities, 147. *See also* calendars

Transportation Safety Administration, 124–25, 140; profiling based on language, 133–35; profiling based on name, 130; profiling of Muslims, 141; profiling of Sikhs, 129, 141. *See also* Islamophobia; September 11th terrorist attacks

Trump v. Hawaii, 105, 136

Trump, Donald J., 134, 136

Truth, Sojourner: "Ain't I A Woman" speech, 81–87

Tulsa Race Massacre, 72

turbans. *See head coverings*

Turner, Nat, 81

United States: and antisemitism, 74; as a Christian nation, 114, 116; Mexico City Policy ("global gag rule"), 114–16; and racism, 72–75; as a white Christian nation, 73–75. *See also* American Empire; First Amendment; September 11th terrorist attacks; US Constitution; US legal system

US Constitution, 73, 106; and equal treatment under the law, 110–12; prohibition on religious tests for office, 105, 136; and right to privacy, 109–12. *See also* First Amendment; Supreme Court, US; *names of specific cases*

US legal system, 100; and Christian nationalism, 100–101, 103, 108, 116; preferential option for white Christianity, 106. *See also* Supreme Court, US; *names of specific cases* violence: fear of, 126, 127; against religious groups, 13, 128

Walmart, 73
War of 1812, 77
War on Terror, 129, 136, 137; Afghanistan War (2001), 129; "axis of evil," 129; Iraq War (2003), 129. *See also* September 11th terrorist attacks
Washington George, 111
white supremacy, 68, 73; and Christianity, 12, 60, 67; and Christian nationalism 99, 108, 115; fears of white decline, 103, 108; imperial creation of, 73; and Islamophobia, 128; Ku Klux Klan, 73; as part of Christian imperial mission, 51; Proud Boys, 73; threats to, 103; and white women's rights, 81–87. *See also* Christian nationalism; prejudice; racism; whiteness
whiteness, 68, 112; creation of, 80; as fundamental to

Americanness, 116; as "moral choice," 80; social benefits of, 67; as systemic privilege, 68; as a tool for justice, 68; as a tool of imperialism, 73. *See also* Christian nationalism; prejudice; racism; white supremacy
world religions paradigm, 28, 36–38, 43; as approach to categorizing, 46; "Big Five" religions, 36, 46; and calendars, 37; and concept of "Muslim world," 51–54; and Indigenous American religion, 87; "major" vs. "minor" religions, 36–37, 46, 95; and mapping, 62; as a tool of imperialism, 36–38, 47; and "Western religions," 52–53

yoga, 14, 17; secularization of, 15

Zitkála Šá, 90
Zoroastrianism, 36; religious observance days, 151. *See also* calendar